DATA PROTECTION ACT 1998

AUSTRALIA
Law Book Co.
Sydney

CANADA and USA
Carswell
Toronto

HONG KONG
Sweet & Maxwell Asia

NEW ZEALAND
Brookers
Wellington

SINGAPORE and MALAYSIA
Sweet & Maxwell Asia
Singapore and Kuala Lumpur

DATA PROTECTION ACT 1998

Annotated by

Emily Wiewiorka

Head of IP/IT Law, Boyds Solicitors

An independent corporate law firm, Boyds was founded in 1955. Well established within the Scottish business community, the firm follows a progressive business strategy. As well as experienced, accredited lawyers on its management team, Boyds has recently embraced non-legal business expertise in order to closely match its skills with the demands of the current commercial climate and specific client requirements.

The firm has offices in Glasgow and Edinburgh, and enjoys a close working relationship with a number of firms in England and world-wide. As a consequence of this national and international network, the depth of knowledge available to its clients ensures that Boyds delivers a high quality service focused on giving practical, comprehensive and relevant advice that is not constrained by locality.

The company currently has 14 partners, offering a broad range of specialisms including Corporate Law and Insolvency, for which it has the second largest dedicated unit in the country, Commercial Property and IP/IT Law.

Emily Wiewiorka is rapidly raising Boyds' profile as a consultative partner to clients looking to develop their e-enabled systems and e-business processes. She is a noted expert in this field from all issues from intellectual property and data protection to national and international contractual issues.

EDINBURGH
W. GREEN/Sweet & Maxwell
2002

Published in 2002 by

W. Green & Son Ltd
21 Alva Street
Edinburgh EH2 4PS

www.wgreen.co.uk

Printed in Great Britain by Athenaeum Press Ltd,
Gateshead, Tyne & Wear

No natural forests were destroyed to make this product;
Only farmed timber was used and replanted

A CIP catalogue record for this book is available from the British Library

ISBN 0414 01467 7

Annotations © Boyds Solicitors 2002

ACKNOWLEDGMENTS

Grateful thanks to Laura Gordon, Boyds, who spent many hours assisting in the preparation of the annotations.

CONTENTS

DATA PROTECTION ACT 1998

(1998 c. 29)

1

An Act to make new provision for the regulation of the processing of information relating to individuals, including the obtaining, holding, use or disclosure of such information.   [16th July 1998]

PART I

PRELIMINARY

Basic interpretative provisions

1.—(1) In this Act, unless the context otherwise requires—
"data" means information which—
    (a) is being processed by means of equipment operating automatically in response to instructions given for that purpose,

(b) is recorded with the intention that it should be processed by means of such equipment,

(c) is recorded as part of a relevant filing system or with the intention that it should form part of a relevant filing system, or

(d) does not fall within paragraph (a), (b) or (c) but forms part of an accessible record as defined by section 68;

"data controller" means, subject to subsection (4), a person who (either alone or jointly or in common with other persons) determines the purposes for which and the manner in which any personal data are, or are to be, processed;

"data processor", in relation to personal data, means any person (other than an employee of the data controller) who processes the data on behalf of the data controller;

"data subject" means an individual who is the subject of personal data;

"personal data" means data which relate to a living individual who can be identified—

(a) from those data, or

(b) from those data and other information which is in the possession of, or is likely to come into the possession of, the data controller,

and includes any expression of opinion about the individual and any indication of the intentions of the data controller or any other person in respect of the individual;

"processing", in relation to information or data, means obtaining, recording or holding the information or data or carrying out any operation or set of operations on the information or data, including—

(a) organisation, adaptation or alteration of the information or data,

(b) retrieval, consultation or use of the information or data,

(c) disclosure of the information or data by transmission, dissemination or otherwise making available, or

(d) alignment, combination, blocking, erasure or destruction of the information or data;

"relevant filing system" means any set of information relating to individuals to the extent that, although the information is not processed by means of equipment operating automatically in response to instructions given for that purpose, the set is structured, either by reference to individuals or by reference to criteria relating to individuals, in such a way that specific information relating to a particular individual is readily accessible.

(2) In this Act, unless the context otherwise requires—

(a) "obtaining" or "recording", in relation to personal data, includes obtaining or recording the information to be contained in the data, and

(b) "using" or "disclosing", in relation to personal data, includes using or disclosing the information contained in the data.

(3) In determining for the purposes of this Act whether any information is recorded with the intention—

(a) that it should be processed by means of equipment operating automatically in response to instructions given for that purpose, or

(b) that it should form part of a relevant filing system,

it is immaterial that it is intended to be so processed or to form part of such a system only after being transferred to a country or territory outside the European Economic Area.

(4) Where personal data are processed only for purposes for which they are required by or under any enactment to be processed, the person on whom the obligation to process the data is imposed by or under that enactment is for the purposes of this Act the data controller.

GENERAL NOTE

Subs. (1)

This subsection defines the key provisions to the Act, with further definitions set out in section 70, followed by an index of all defined expressions in section 71. All definitions within the Act must be read in conjunction with the other definitions.

"**Data**" means information which:

(a) is being processed automatically. Although "equipment operating automatically" relates to computers and other electronic devices containing micro-circuits, the word "computer" is not mentioned in the Act. However, this definition also includes devices such as CCTV cameras. Those in control of CCTV cameras are data controllers and notices should be placed in prominent positions advising data subjects of the fact that CCTV cameras are in operation.

(b) is recorded with the intention that it will be processed automatically. For example, personal information collected on questionnaire forms or street surveys with the intention of downloading this information on computer at a later date is covered by the Act.

(c) is recorded in a relevant filing system. This applies to certain manual records provided that the files are structured affording individuals easy access to the personal data.

(d) forms part of an accessible record. "Accessible record" is defined in section 68 as health records, educational records and certain public records.

A "**data controller**" is any person who (either alone or with others) makes decisions regarding personal data. This person determines the purposes for which and the manner in which any personal data are processed. It is important to establish whether or not someone is a data controller because the Act requires data controllers to comply with the *Data Protection Principles*.

A data controller must be a legal person, and includes individuals, as well as organisations such as companies and other corporate and unincorporated bodies.

It is possible for there to be more than one data controller processing personal data, and therefore data controllers can act jointly or in common with others in this respect. Jointly in this respect means when two or more data controllers act together in determining the purposes and manner of processing. In common means that the personal data are shared, with each data controller acting independently of each other.

A "**data processor**" is any person who processes personal data on behalf of the data controller. This does not include employees of the data controller. It refers to those who have been contracted to process the data.

There are no obligations imposed by the Act on the data processor. The data processor can only process personal data in accordance with instructions received from the data controller and cannot use the personal data for his own purposes.

A "**data subject**" is a living individual who is the subject of personal data. A company cannot be a data subject. Partnerships and sole traders may be data subjects.

"**Personal data**" means data which relates to a living, identifiable individual who can be identified from the data, or from any other information in the possession of, or likely to be in the possession of the data controller.

Information may relate to an individual in a business capacity. Although the Act applies to individuals and not companies, if a data controller holds information about contacts within a company, this will be personal data.

The definition of personal data is extremely wide and includes photographs scanned into a computer, soundtracks, mailing lists and even DNA samples or fingerprints.

Examples of personal data:

(1) The capture of an image of an individual by a CCTV camera may be done in such a way that distinguishable features of that individual are processed and identified from the captured images. This is classed as personal data.

(2) In the context of the internet, many e-mail addresses are personal data as the e-mail address clearly identifies a particular individual, for example john.smith@hotmail.com.

"**Processing**" is widely defined within the Act and applies to all processing activities from collection to destruction of data. It includes any operations that are carried out in respect of data or information, and is not limited to processing of personal data or information relating to a specific individual. Note that the disclosure of personal data by a data controller amounts to processing under the Act.

"**Relevant filing system**" relates to manual filing systems caught by the Act. In order for manual files to be caught by the Act, they must meet the following criteria:

(a) there must be a set of information relating to individuals;

(b) which is structured either by reference to individuals or by criteria relating to individuals;

(c) in such a way that specific information relating to particular individuals is readily accessible.

Manual files caught by the Act do not need to be stored in the same filing cabinet, or even the same building or city, so long as together the files form a set of information within the meaning of the definition.

The extent of the definition has been the subject of much discussion between the Information Commissioner and the Government, and it is considered that much will turn on how "ready accessibility" is interpreted by the Information Commissioner, the Tribunal, the courts and the European Commission. If manual files are structured internally, these files are caught by the Act. Miscellaneous collections of documents contained within a manual file should not be caught.

Subs. (2)

In this context, and in general throughout the Act, the terms "obtaining" and "recording" will apply to information which, whilst not obtained or recorded in the form of personal data, is intended to be used as personal data.

Therefore, if information is obtained or recorded which does not identify a living individual, but which is then placed with other information that does identify a living individual, it should be treated as personal data.

The terms "using" or "disclosing" will generally apply to information which, whilst it is not being used or disclosed in the form of personal data, is derived from it.

Subs. (3)

The effect of this subsection is to prevent a person recording information within the European Economic Area (EEA) and then transferring it out of the EEA where it may be processed or incorporated into a relevant filing system, in order to avoid the obligations imposed by the Data Protection Directive. The EEA comprises the European Union Member States, plus Norway, Iceland and Liechtenstein.

Sensitive personal data

2. In this Act "sensitive personal data" means personal data consisting of information as to—

   (a) the racial or ethnic origin of the data subject,

   (b) his political opinions,

   (c) his religious beliefs or other beliefs of a similar nature,

   (d) whether he is a member of a trade union (within the meaning of the Trade Union and Labour Relations (Consolidation) Act 1992),

   (e) his physical or mental health or condition,

   (f) his sexual life,

   (g) the commission or alleged commission by him of any offence, or

   (h) any proceedings for any offence committed or alleged to have been committed by him, the disposal of such proceedings or the sentence of any court in such proceedings.

GENERAL NOTE

This section defines "sensitive personal data".

It provides that personal data that falls within one of the categories contained in this section shall be regarded as sensitive personal data. Sensitive personal data means personal data consisting of information as to:

   (a) The racial or ethnic origin of the data subject. This will include the colour of an individual but not necessarily his nationality. It was expressed in the House of Lords debates during the Bill's progress through Parliament that "data about nationality are not of the same sensitivity as data relating to racial or ethnic origin". Whether or not nationality reveals racial or ethnic origin depends upon the circumstances. This is supported by the Race Relations Act 1976, s.3(1), which defines "racial grounds" as any of the following: "colour, race, nationality or ethnic or national origins".

   (b) The political opinions of the data subject. Political opinion has not yet been judicially defined. However, the word "political" was considered in *R. v. Radio Authority, ex parte Bull* [1995] 4 All E.R. 481 where the authority rejected an advertisement placed by Amnesty International because of its political nature. The court construed the word "political" as pertaining to the policy of the Government and wider than the definition of party political.

(c) The religious beliefs or other beliefs of a similar nature of the data subject. This does not include philosophical beliefs. "Religious beliefs" was discussed in *Barralet v. Attorney-General* [1980] 3 All E.R. 918 in which it was held that faith in God and worship of that God by submission, veneration, praise, thanks-giving or prayer were essential attributes of religion. There could be no worship in that sense of ethical or philosophical ideas.

(d) Whether the data subject is a member of a trade union (within the meaning of the Trade Union and Labour Relations (Consolidation) Act 1992). A person becomes a member of a trade union when his application for membership is accepted in accordance with the rules of the trade union. "Trade Union" is defined in section 1 of the Trade Union and Labour Relations (Consolidation) Act 1992. Only trade union membership and not membership of any other type of professional body or trade organisation is subject to the additional safeguards that are afforded to sensitive personal data because of the discrimination that trade union members have suffered in the past.

(e) A data subject's physical or mental health or condition. Sensitive personal data also covers health conditions which do not display symptoms and which may not appear or affect a person's health until some time in the future. It may also cover information showing that a person has a pre-disposition towards a particular type of health problem. This is intended to cover genetic data. Personal data in respect of an individual's physical or mental health or condition need not necessarily be in respect of ill health. A pregnant woman or a person who was born blind may both have a physical condition but neither is suffering from ill health. Therefore, a description of a person's general good health and fitness is also sensitive personal data under the Act.

(f) A data subject's sexual life. This includes the data subject's sexual orientation and marital status.

(g) The commission or alleged commission by a data subject of an offence; and

(h) Any proceedings for any offence committed or alleged to have been committed by a data subject, the disposal of such proceedings or the sentence of any court in such proceedings. Both categories (g) and (h) were fairly controversial when their inclusion was discussed during the passing of the Bill through the House of Commons and the House of Lords, as the Directive does not include them as sensitive personal data. However, the Directive requires that data and information that relates to a person's criminal record should only be processed under official authority or with specific safeguards in place. The effect of their inclusion as sensitive personal data means that processing of data with regard to a person's criminal record will require compliance with one of the conditions in Schedule 2 and Schedule 3.

The special purposes

3. In this Act "the special purposes" means any one or more of the following—

(a) the purposes of journalism,

(b) artistic purposes, and

(c) literary purposes.

GENERAL NOTE

The Act makes special provision where personal data is processed for special purposes. "Special purposes", which is used throughout the Act, is defined to mean any one or more of the following:

(a) the purposes of journalism;

(b) artistic purposes; and

(c) literary purposes.

The Data Protection Act 1984 provided no exemptions, for example, for journalists, who were required to comply with the regulations with regard to processing and access to data. The Act provides wide exemptions for the special purposes defined above, namely where processing takes place with a view to publication and where the data controller believes that publication would be in the public interest.

The words "journalist" and "journalism" are not statutorily defined, and their meaning is likely to be the subject of considerable debate.

Although "artistic purposes" are not defined in the Act, an "artistic work" is defined in the Copyright, Designs and Patents Act 1988. This definition includes a graphic work, as well as a photograph, sculpture or collage, or a work of architecture or artistic craftsmanship. Therefore, when personal data are processed to produce a photograph or map, the personal data will be considered to be processed for the special purposes, and therefore subject to the exemptions contained in section 32. Section 3(1) of the Copyright Act also defines a "literary work" to include any work, other than a dramatic or musical work, or one which is written, spoken or sung. It includes tables, compilations and computer programs.

The data protection principles

4.—(1) References in this Act to the data protection principles are to the principles set out in Part I of Schedule 1.

(2) Those principles are to be interpreted in accordance with Part II of Schedule 1.

(3) Schedule 2 (which applies to all personal data) and Schedule 3 (which applies only to sensitive personal data) set out conditions applying for the purposes of the first principle; and Schedule 4 sets out cases in which the eighth principle does not apply.

(4) Subject to section 27(1), it shall be the duty of a data controller to comply with the data protection principles in relation to all personal data with respect to which he is the data controller.

GENERAL NOTE

The eight data protection principles are contained in Part I of Schedule 1 to the Act. The principles are to be interpreted in accordance with Part II of Schedule 1.

At least one condition in Schedule 2 must be satisfied before any personal data are processed.

In addition, at least one condition in Schedule 3 must be satisfied when any sensitive personal data are processed.

Schedule 4 sets out exceptions to the principle that personal data must not be transferred outside the European Economic Area (EEA) unless the country or territory to which it is transferred ensures an adequate level of protection for the rights and freedoms of data subjects in relation to the processing of personal data. Countries that are considered to provide adequate protection will be subject to a "Community Finding" allowing European Union data controllers to transfer data to those states without further consideration of the adequacy of protection. At February 2001, the European Commission has adopted a "Decision" to the effect that Switzerland and Hungary provide adequate protection. To check the approved list of countries visit the office of the Information Commissioner's web site at www.dataprotection.gov.uk.

Subs. (4)

A data controller has a statutory obligation to comply with the data protection principles in relation to all personal data of which it is the data controller unless it is exempted from doing so under Part IV of the Act.

Application of Act

5.—(1) Except as otherwise provided by or under section 54, this Act applies to a data controller in respect of any data only if—

    (a) the data controller is established in the United Kingdom and the data are processed in the context of that establishment, or

    (b) the data controller is established neither in the United Kingdom nor in any other EEA State but uses equipment in the United Kingdom for processing the data otherwise than for the purposes of transit through the United Kingdom.

(2) A data controller falling within subsection (1)(b) must nominate for the purposes of this Act a representative established in the United Kingdom.

(3) For the purposes of subsections (1) and (2), each of the following is to be treated as established in the United Kingdom—

    (a) an individual who is ordinarily resident in the United Kingdom,

    (b) a body incorporated under the law of, or of any part of, the United Kingdom,

    (c) a partnership or other unincorporated association formed under the law of any part of the United Kingdom, and

(d) any person who does not fall within paragraph (a), (b) or (c) but maintains in the United Kingdom—

(i) an office, branch or agency through which he carries on any activity, or

(ii) a regular practice;

and the reference to establishment in any other EEA State has a corresponding meaning.

GENERAL NOTE

This section determines the jurisdiction of the Act. The Act only applies to data controllers established in the United Kingdom. The meaning of "established" is defined in subsection (3) as an individual who is ordinarily resident in the United Kingdom, a body incorporated under United Kingdom law or a partnership or unincorporated association formed under United Kingdom law.

The Act applies where the processing is carried out by a data controller established in the United Kingdom, whether or not the data is actually processed in the United Kingdom, in another Member State or elsewhere.

The Act also applies to data controllers who are not established within the United Kingdom or European Economic Area (EEA) but who use equipment in the United Kingdom for processing data. This does not include data which is merely in transit and which is not being processed in the United Kingdom. In this case, data controllers must appoint a representative in the United Kingdom who will be subject to the provisions of the Act.

This section is subject to the provisions of section 54 which imposes obligations upon the Information Commissioner in respect of international co-operation.

The Commissioner and the Tribunal

6.—'(1) For the purposes of this Act and of the Freedom of Information Act 2000 there shall be an officer known as the Information Commissioner (in this Act referred to as "the Commissioner").

(2) The Commissioner shall be appointed by Her Majesty by Letters Patent.

'(3) For the purposes of this Act and of the Freedom of Information Act 2000 there shall be a tribunal known as the Information Tribunal (in this Act referred to as "the Tribunal").

(4) The Tribunal shall consist of—

(a) a chairman appointed by the Lord Chancellor after consultation with the Lord Advocate,

(b) such number of deputy chairmen so appointed as the Lord Chancellor may determine, and

(c) such number of other members appointed by the Secretary of State as he may determine.

(5) The members of the Tribunal appointed under subsection (4)(a) and (b) shall be—

(a) persons who have a 7 year general qualification, within the meaning of section 71 of the Courts and Legal Services Act 1990,

(b) advocates or solicitors in Scotland of at least 7 years' standing, or

(c) members of the bar of Northern Ireland or solicitors of the Supreme Court of Northern Ireland of at least 7 years' standing.

(6) The members of the Tribunal appointed under subsection (4)(c) shall be—

(a) persons to represent the interests of data subjects,

'(aa) persons to represent the interests of those who make requests for information under the Freedom of Information Act 2000,

(b) persons to represent the interests of data controllers, and

'(bb) persons to represent the interests of public authorities.

(7) Schedule 5 has effect in relation to the Commissioner and the Tribunal.

NOTE
[1] Substituted by the Freedom of Information Act 2000 (c.36), Sched. 2, para. 13(2).
[2] Substituted by the Freedom of Information Act 2000 (c.36), Sched. 2, para. 13(3).
[3] Added by the Freedom of Information Act 2000 (c.36), Sched. 2, para. 16(a).
[4] Added by the Freedom of Information Act 2000 (c.36), Sched. 2, para. 16(b).

GENERAL NOTE

Subsections (1) to (3) establish the Commissioner and the Data Protection Tribunal. The Commissioner was formerly known as "The Data Protection Registrar" under the 1984 Act. It should be noted that the Freedom of Information Act 2000 amended section 6(1) of the Act. This amendment means that, as of January 30, 2001, the "Office of the Data Protection Commissioner" is now known as the "Office of the Information Commissioner", and the Commissioner is now known as the "Information Commissioner". The powers of the Commissioner and the Tribunal are set out in Schedule 5 along with the terms of their appointment, salary, officers, staff and other matters.

Subsections (4) to (6) refer to the Tribunal which consists of a legally qualified chairman and deputy chairmen along with other members who may or may not be legally qualified and will be appointed to represent the interests of data subjects and data controllers.

PART II

RIGHTS OF DATA SUBJECTS AND OTHERS

Right of access to personal data

'7.—(1) Subject to the following provisions of this section and to sections 8 and 9, an individual is entitled—
  (a) to be informed by any data controller whether personal data of which that individual is the data subject are being processed by or on behalf of that data controller,
  (b) if that is the case, to be given by the data controller a description of—
      (i) the personal data of which that individual is the data subject,
      (ii) the purposes for which they are being or are to be processed, and
      (iii) the recipients or classes of recipients to whom they are or may be disclosed,
  (c) to have communicated to him in an intelligible form—
      (i) the information constituting any personal data of which that individual is the data subject, and
      (ii) any information available to the data controller as to the source of those data, and
  (d) where the processing by automatic means of personal data of which that individual is the data subject for the purpose of evaluating matters relating to him such as, for example, his performance at work, his credit worthiness, his reliability or his conduct, has constituted or is likely to constitute the sole basis for any decision significantly affecting him, to be informed by the data controller of the logic involved in that decision-taking.

(2) A data controller is not obliged to supply any information under subsection (1) unless he has received—
  (a) a request in writing, and
  (b) except in prescribed cases, such fee (not exceeding the prescribed maximum) as he may require.

[2](3) Where a data controller—
  (a) reasonably requires further information in order to satisfy himself as to the identity of the person making a request under this section and to locate the information which that person seeks, and

(b) has informed him of that requirement,

the data controller is not obliged to comply with the request unless he is supplied with that further information.

(4) Where a data controller cannot comply with the request without disclosing information relating to another individual who can be identified from that information, he is not obliged to comply with the request unless—

(a) the other individual has consented to the disclosure of the information to the person making the request, or

(b) it is reasonable in all the circumstances to comply with the request without the consent of the other individual.

(5) In subsection (4) the reference to information relating to another individual includes a reference to information identifying that individual as the source of the information sought by the request; and that subsection is not to be construed as excusing a data controller from communicating so much of the information sought by the request as can be communicated without disclosing the identity of the other individual concerned, whether by the omission of names or other identifying particulars or otherwise.

(6) In determining for the purposes of subsection (4)(b) whether it is reasonable in all the circumstances to comply with the request without the consent of the other individual concerned, regard shall be had, in particular, to—

(a) any duty of confidentiality owed to the other individual,

(b) any steps taken by the data controller with a view to seeking the consent of the other individual,

(c) whether the other individual is capable of giving consent, and

(d) any express refusal of consent by the other individual.

(7) An individual making a request under this section may, in such cases as may be prescribed, specify that his request is limited to personal data of any prescribed description.

(8) Subject to subsection (4), a data controller shall comply with a request under this section promptly and in any event before the end of the prescribed period beginning with the relevant day.

(9) If a court is satisfied on the application of any person who has made a request under the foregoing provisions of this section that the data controller in question has failed to comply with the request in contravention of those provisions, the court may order him to comply with the request.

(10) In this section—

"prescribed" means prescribed by the Secretary of State by regulations:

"the prescribed maximum" means such amount as may be prescribed:

"the prescribed period" means forty days or such other period as may be prescribed:

"the relevant day", in relation to a request under this section, means the day on which the data controller receives the request or, if later, the first day on which the data controller has both the required fee and the information referred to in subsection (3).

(11) Different amounts or periods may be prescribed under this section in relation to different cases.[2]

Notes

[1]This section is modified in relation to data to which the Data Protection (Subject Access Modification) (Health) Order 2000, Data Protection (Subject Access Modification) (Education) Order 2000, and para. 1 of Sched. 1 to the Data Protection (Subject Access Modification) (Social Work) Order 2000 applies. See those provisions for applicable modifications.

[2]Substituted by the Freedom of Information Act 2000 (c.36), Sched. 6, para. 1.

GENERAL NOTE

Subs. (1)

This subsection sets out the right of access to personal data. Paragraphs (a) to (d) detail the personal data that must be disclosed when a data subject makes a subject information request.

Section 7(1)(a) entitles a data subject to be informed whether a data controller or data processor on behalf of the data controller is processing personal data about that data subject. If this is the case then the subject access provisions will apply.

Section 7(1)(b) provides that a data subject is entitled to be given a description of:
   (i) the personal data;
   (ii) the purposes for processing that personal data; and
   (iii) a list of the recipients of the data.

The data subject is also entitled to have communicated to him:
   (i) the information constituting any personal data of which he is the subject; and
   (ii) any information available to the data controller as to the source of the data (section 7(1)(c)).

The term "intelligible" referred to in section 7(1)(c) is not defined in the Act. Where personal data contains abbreviations or jargon that cannot be understood without an accompanying explanation, the data controller should provide an explanation of those abbreviations or jargon. This also applies where data is encrypted.

With regard to information as to the source of the data, this need only be provided if it is available to the data controller. Later sections place further restrictions on disclosure of information identifying the source of personal data, particularly where such information would reveal the identity of a third party (section 7(3)–(6)).

Under section 7(1)(d), a data controller must inform an individual of the logic involved in any decision taken by automatic means for the purpose of evaluating matters relating to him, for example his performance at work or his creditworthiness. This requirement only applies where automatic processing of data constitutes, or is likely to constitute, the sole basis of any decision. A data controller is not obliged to supply this information unless the request is made in writing (which includes transmission by electronic means), and the prescribed fee has been paid. The data controller has the right to waive the fee.

Subs. (3)

This subsection states that a data controller is not obliged to comply with a request for information unless sufficient information is supplied allowing the data controller to be satisfied as to the identity of the person making the subject access request. The data controller must also be able to locate the information requested.

Subss. (4) to (6)

Section 7(4) deals with circumstances where disclosure of personal data would lead to disclosure of information relating to a third party. In such a case, a data controller is not obliged to comply with a request unless the third party has consented to the disclosure of information or it is reasonable in the circumstances to comply with the request without the consent of the third party.

This improves upon the position under the 1984 Act, which was that a data user was not obliged to disclose personal data relating to a third party unless the third party had consented to the disclosure. It was enacted to reflect the decision in *Gaskin* [1990] 1 F.L.R. 167, a European Court of Human Rights case concerning access to medical records.

Section 7(5) clarifies that the phrase "information relating to another individual" in subsection (4) includes any information identifying that individual as the source of the data sought. However, the subsection also makes it clear that a data controller is obliged to provide as much personal data as it is able to without disclosing the identity of any third party.

Factors to be taken into consideration in determining whether it is reasonable to comply with a request without the consent of a third party set out in section 7(6) include:
   (a) any duty of confidentiality owed to the third party;
   (b) any steps the data controller has taken to obtain the consent of the third party;
   (c) whether the third party is capable of giving consent to the disclosure; and
   (d) any express refusal of consent by the third party.

Subs. (7)

Although section 7(7) provides that an individual making a request can specify that the request is limited to personal data of a prescribed description, this right is not yet available in practice. The Secretary of State has the power to allow the data subject to limit his request in this way.

Subs. (8)

This subsection places time constraints on a data controller by requiring him to comply with a subject access request promptly and in any event before the end of the prescribed period. The "prescribed period" is defined in section 7(10) as forty days unless otherwise prescribed by the Secretary of State. The time limit will start to run from the day on which the data controller receives the request in writing, or if later, the day on which the data controller receives the prescribed fee (currently £10, at the discretion of the data controller) and any information necessary to identify the data subject and locate the information requested.

Section 7(8) is however qualified by paragraph 8 of Schedule 7 that puts in place provisions to ensure that examination marks are not disclosed in response to a subject access request before their official publication date.

Subs. (9)

In accordance with section 7(9), a court may order a data controller to comply with a request for information. It may also award compensation in certain circumstances contained in section 13. However, under section 8(3), if a data controller has previously complied with a request, he is not obliged to comply with a subsequent request unless a reasonable time period has elapsed between the requests. Section 8(4) provides guidance as to what is meant by reasonable interval. The data controller should take account of the nature of the data, the purpose of the processing of that personal data and the frequency of alteration of the personal data.

Subs. (10)

This subsection is an interpretation section and contains definitions of the terms used in section 7. They are discussed in relation to each relevant subsection above.

Provisions supplementary to section 7

8.—(1) The Secretary of State may by regulations provide that, in such cases as may be prescribed, a request for information under any provision of subsection (1) of section 7 is to be treated as extending also to information under other provisions of that subsection.

(2) The obligation imposed by section 7(1)(c)(i) must be complied with by supplying the data subject with a copy of the information in permanent form unless—

(a) the supply of such a copy is not possible or would involve disproportionate effort, or

(b) the data subject agrees otherwise;

and where any of the information referred to in section 7(1)(c)(i) is expressed in terms which are not intelligible without explanation the copy must be accompanied by an explanation of those terms.

(3) Where a data controller has previously complied with a request made under section 7 by an individual, the data controller is not obliged to comply with a subsequent identical or similar request under that section by that individual unless a reasonable interval has elapsed between compliance with the previous request and the making of the current request.

(4) In determining for the purposes of subsection (3) whether requests under section 7 are made at reasonable intervals, regard shall be had to the nature of the data, the purposes for which the data are processed and the frequency with which the data are altered.

(5) Section 7(1)(d) is not to be regarded as requiring the provision of information as to the logic involved in any decision-taking if, and to the extent that, the information constitutes a trade secret.

(6) The information to be supplied pursuant to a request under section 7 must be supplied by reference to the data in question at the time when the request is received, except that it may take account of any amendment or deletion made between that time and the time when the information is supplied, being an amendment or deletion that would have been made regardless of the receipt of the request.

(7) For the purposes of section 7(4) and (5) another individual can be identified from the information being disclosed if he can be identified from

that information, or from that and any other information which, in the reasonable belief of the data controller, is likely to be in, or to come into, the possession of the data subject making the request.

GENERAL NOTE

Subs. (1)

Under section 8(1), the Secretary of State may make an order that any request for information under section 7(1) shall be taken to extend to information under other provisions of that subsection. Section 7(1) contains far wider categories of information than the 1984 Act with the result that it is easier and cheaper for a data subject to exercise his rights of access.

Subs. (2)

This subsection requires the description of the information referred to in section 7(1)(c) to be provided in permanent form. The information does not have to be provided in a permanent form if it would involve a "disproportionate effort" to do so, or the data subject agrees to be provided with information in another form (for example, by visiting the data controller's premises and viewing it on screen).

The Act does not provide a definition of "disproportionate effort", but this phrase is likely to be interpreted in accordance with the principle of proportionality and reasonableness particularly as the Act is not intended to place an unnecessary burden on data controllers.

Subs. (3)

This subsection provides that a data controller does not have to comply with a request for information that is similar or identical to a previous request. However, this does not apply where a reasonable interval has elapsed between compliance with the previous request and the making of the current request.

Subs. (4)

This subsection provides guidance as to what is meant by "reasonable interval". A data controller must consider the nature of the data concerned, the purpose for which the data are being processed and the frequency with which the data have been altered. This suggests that a data subject would be able to make frequent requests for data which are being constantly amended.

Subs. (5)

This subsection qualifies the right to access to the logic of the decision, by providing that information as to the logic of the decision does not require to be provided where that information constitutes a trade secret.

Subs. (6)

This subsection sets out the rule that the information to be supplied in response to a request is the information which was in existence at the time of receipt of the request. However, the subsection also provides that a data controller may continue to make changes to the data between the time of receipt of the request and the time the information is supplied if such change would have been made regardless of the notice.

Application of section 7 where data controller is credit reference agency

9.—(1) Where the data controller is a credit reference agency, section 7 has effect subject to the provisions of this section.

(2) An individual making a request under section 7 may limit his request to personal data relevant to his financial standing, and shall be taken to have so limited his request unless the request shows a contrary intention.

(3) Where the data controller receives a request under section 7 in a case where personal data of which the individual making the request is the data subject are being processed by or on behalf of the data controller, the obligation to supply information under that section includes an obligation to give the individual making the request a statement, in such form as may be prescribed by the Secretary of State by regulations, of the individual's rights—

(a) under section 159 of the Consumer Credit Act 1974, and

(b) to the extent required by the prescribed form, under this Act.

GENERAL NOTE
This section brings about a change in the position in relation to obtaining information from a credit reference agency. Under the 1984 Act, this type of information was exempt from the subject access provisions.

Subs. (1)
Under section 9(1), section 7 applies where a data controller is a credit reference agency. However, the application of section 7 to credit reference agencies is qualified by the provisions of subsection (2).

Subs. (2)
Under section 9(2), an individual making a request to a credit reference agency is limited to information relating to his financial standing only.

Subs. (3)
This subsection ensures that data controllers supply a statement of the data subject's rights under section 159 of the Consumer Credit Act 1974, when providing information requested under section 7. Section 9(3) further allows the Secretary of State to prescribe the form of this statement at a later date.

Right to prevent processing likely to cause damage or distress

10.—(1) Subject to subsection (2), an individual is entitled at any time by notice in writing to a data controller to require the data controller at the end of such period as is reasonable in the circumstances to cease, or not to begin, processing, or processing for a specified purpose or in a specified manner, any personal data in respect of which he is the data subject, on the ground that, for specified reasons—

    (a) the processing of those data or their processing for that purpose or in that manner is causing or is likely to cause substantial damage or substantial distress to him or to another, and

    (b) that damage or distress is or would be unwarranted.

(2) Subsection (1) does not apply—

    (a) in a case where any of the conditions in paragraphs 1 to 4 of Schedule 2 is met, or

    (b) in such other cases as may be prescribed by the Secretary of State by order.

(3) The data controller must within twenty-one days of receiving a notice under subsection (1) ("the data subject notice") give the individual who gave it a written notice—

    (a) stating that he has complied or intends to comply with the data subject notice, or

    (b) stating his reasons for regarding the data subject notice as to any extent unjustified and the extent (if any) to which he has complied or intends to comply with it.

(4) If a court is satisfied, on the application of any person who has given a notice under subsection (1) which appears to the court to be justified (or to be justified to any extent), that the data controller in question has failed to comply with the notice, the court may order him to take such steps for complying with the notice (or for complying with it to that extent) as the court thinks fit.

(5) The failure by a data subject to exercise the right conferred by subsection (1) or section 11(1) does not affect any other right conferred on him by this Part.

GENERAL NOTE

Subss. (1) and (2)
Under section 10(1), an individual has the right to prevent a data controller processing personal data (either new or existing). Such notice should be in writing and cessation may be requested on

the grounds that the processing of the data is causing or is likely to cause unwarranted or substantial damage or distress to the data subject.

The terms "substantial" and "unwarranted" are not defined in the Act. The courts application of this section will determine how narrowly or widely these terms are construed.

Important exemptions to this right are set out in section 10(2). The right will not apply where:

(a) the data subject has consented to the processing;
(b) the processing is necessary for the entering into or performing of a contract with the data subject;
(c) the processing must be carried out in order to comply with a legal obligation (other than a contractual one);
(d) it is vital in the interests of the data subject that the data are processed; or
(e) it is prescribed by the Secretary of State.

Subs. (3)

This subsection obliges a data controller to respond to a data subject's notice within 21 days stating whether or not it intends to comply with the request. If a data controller intends to continue processing either all or some of the information, it must inform the data subject of its reasons for doing so.

Subs. (4)

This subsection details the data subject's right to apply to the court for an order requiring the data controller to comply with the request.

Right to prevent processing for purposes of direct marketing

11.—(1) An individual is entitled at any time by notice in writing to a data controller to require the data controller at the end of such period as is reasonable in the circumstances to cease, or not to begin, processing for the purposes of direct marketing personal data in respect of which he is the data subject.

(2) If the court is satisfied, on the application of any person who has given a notice under subsection (1), that the data controller has failed to comply with the notice, the court may order him to take such steps for complying with the notice as the court thinks fit.

'(2A) This section shall not apply in relation to the processing of such data as are mentioned in paragraph (1) of regulation 8 of the Telecommunications (Data Protection and Privacy) Regulations 1999 (processing of telecommunications billing data for certain marketing purposes) for the purposes mentioned in paragraph (2) of that regulation.

(3) In this section "direct marketing" means the communication (by whatever means) of any advertising or marketing material which is directed to particular individuals.

NOTE

[1]Added by Telecommunications (Data Protection and Privacy) Regulations 1999 (S.I. 1999 No. 2093), Sched. 1(II), para. 3.

GENERAL NOTE

Subs. (1)

Subsection (1) grants to a data subject the right to prevent processing (either new or existing) of his personal data for direct marketing purposes. This puts in place a specific right that was only indirectly provided by the 1984 Act.

This right is more extensive than the right to prevent processing under section 10 and the right to prevent automated decision-making under section 12. The right to prevent processing for direct marketing purposes is absolute and is not subject to any qualifications.

Subs. (3)

This subsection defines direct marketing as the communication (by any means) of advertising or marketing material that is directed to particular individuals. This broad definition would therefore include marketing by e-mail, telephone and door-to-door canvassing, but would not appear to apply to mail shots addressed simply to "the occupier".

Rights in relation to automated decision-taking

12.—(1) An individual is entitled at any time, by notice in writing to any data controller, to require the data controller to ensure that no decision taken by or on behalf of the data controller which significantly affects that individual is based solely on the processing by automatic means of personal data in respect of which that individual is the data subject for the purpose of evaluating matters relating to him such as, for example, his performance at work, his credit worthiness, his reliability or his conduct.

(2) Where, in a case where no notice under subsection (1) has effect, a decision which significantly affects an individual is based solely on such processing as is mentioned in subsection (1)—

(a) the data controller must as soon as reasonably practicable notify the individual that the decision was taken on that basis, and

(b) the individual is entitled, within twenty-one days of receiving that notification from the data controller, by notice in writing to require the data controller to reconsider the decision or to take a new decision otherwise than on that basis.

(3) The data controller must, within twenty-one days of receiving a notice under subsection (2)(b) ("the data subject notice") give the individual a written notice specifying the steps that he intends to take to comply with the data subject notice.

(4) A notice under subsection (1) does not have effect in relation to an exempt decision; and nothing in subsection (2) applies to an exempt decision.

(5) In subsection (4) "exempt decision" means any decision—

(a) in respect of which the condition in subsection (6) and the condition in subsection (7) are met, or

(b) which is made in such other circumstances as may be prescribed by the Secretary of State by order.

(6) The condition in this subsection is that the decision—

(a) is taken in the course of steps taken—

(i) for the purpose of considering whether to enter into a contract with the data subject,

(ii) with a view to entering into such a contract, or

(iii) in the course of performing such a contract, or

(b) is authorised or required by or under any enactment.

(7) The condition in this subsection is that either—

(a) the effect of the decision is to grant a request of the data subject, or

(b) steps have been taken to safeguard the legitimate interests of the data subject (for example, by allowing him to make representations).

(8) If a court is satisfied on the application of a data subject that a person taking a decision in respect of him ("the responsible person") has failed to comply with subsection (1) or (2)(b), the court may order the responsible person to reconsider the decision, or to take a new decision which is not based solely on such processing as is mentioned in subsection (1).

(9) An order under subsection (8) shall not affect the rights of any person other than the data subject and the responsible person.

GENERAL NOTE

Subs. (1)

Subsection (1) entitles an individual to prevent certain decisions being taken about him solely by automatic means. This entitlement only applies to decisions that significantly affect the individual and are taken in relation to important matters relating to him, for example, his credit worthiness.

Subs. (2)

This subsection deals with a situation where notice served under section 12(1) has no effect (for example, where a decision has already been taken). It obliges the data controller to inform the individual as soon as is reasonably practicable that the decision was taken by automatic means. Furthermore, the individual has the right to require the data controller to reconsider the decision or to take a new decision, provided that the individual exercises this right within 21 days of the initial decision.

Subs. (3)

This subsection requires the data controller, within 21 days of receiving a notice under section 12(2), to give the individual concerned a written notice detailing the steps it plans to take in order to comply with the request.

Subss. (4) to (7)

These subsections limit the individual's right of objection to decisions taken by automated means where that decision can be classified as "exempt".

An "exempt decision" is defined as a decision:

    (a) taken in order to enter into or perform a contract with the data subject or a decision authorised or required by law; and

    (b) the effect of the decision is either to grant a request of the data subject, or where no request is granted, the data subject's legitimate interests are safeguarded (for example, by providing an appeal procedure against the decision).

Where a decision is classified as exempt, the data controller does not have to comply with the requirements of section 12(2).

Rights of data subjects in relation to exempt manual data

12A.'— Rights of data subjects in relation to exempt manual data.

(1) A data subject is entitled at any time by notice in writing—

    (a) to require the data controller to rectify, block, erase or destroy exempt manual data which are inaccurate or incomplete, or

    (b) to require the data controller to cease holding exempt manual data in a way incompatible with the legitimate purposes pursued by the data controller.

(2) A notice under subsection (1)(a) or (b) must state the data subject's reasons for believing that the data are inaccurate or incomplete or, as the case may be, his reasons for believing that they are held in a way incompatible with the legitimate purposes pursued by the data controller.

(3) If the court is satisfied, on the application of any person who has given a notice under subsection (1) which appears to the court to be justified (or to be justified to any extent) that the data controller in question has failed to comply with the notice, the court may order him to take such steps for complying with the notice (or for complying with it to that extent) as the court thinks fit.

(4) In this section "exempt manual data" means —

    (a) in relation to the first transitional period, as defined by paragraph 1(2) of Schedule 8, data to which paragraph 3 or 4 of that Schedule applies, and

    (b) in relation to the second transitional period, as so defined, data to which paragraph 14 of that Schedule applies.

(5) For the purposes of this section personal data are incomplete if, and only if, the data, although not inaccurate, are such that their incompleteness would constitute a contravention of the third or fourth data protection principles, if those principles applied to the data.

NOTE

'Added by the Data Protection Act 1998 (c.29), Sched. 13, para. 1, effective March 1, 2000.

GENERAL NOTE

This section deals with the rights of data subjects in relation to exempt manual data. A data subject is entitled at any time by notice in writing to require a data controller to either rectify, block, erase or destroy inaccurate or incomplete exempt manual data or cease holding any exempt manual data that is incompatible with the legitimate purposes of the data controller.

Subs. (2) and (3)

Any notice given by the data subject must state his reasons for believing that the exempt manual data falls within either of the above categories.

If a data controller fails to comply with any notice received from a data subject, it is open to the data subject to apply to a court for the court to order the data controller to take such steps as the court thinks reasonable to comply with the notice. This means that the court can either require the data controller to rectify, block, erase or destroy the data or to cease holding the data that is incompatible with the data controller's legitimate purposes.

Subs. (4)

This subsection defines "exempt manual data". Two definitions are set out, the first definition dealing with the period from October 24, 1998 to October 23, 2001. In this first transitional period, exempt manual data meant manually held personal data either forming part of an accessible record (that is, health records, educational records and accessible public records) or consisting of information relevant to the financial standing of the data subject that was already being processed prior to October 24, 1998. The second definition refers to the second transitional period, that is, the period from October 24, 2001 to October 23, 2007. Exempt manual data in this second transitional period means all manual data (excluding manual data processed only for the purpose of historical research in compliance with the relevant conditions set out in section 33) already being processed prior to October 24, 1998.

Subs. (5)

"Incomplete" personal data means that although the personal data is not inaccurate, their "incompleteness" would contravene the third principle (personal data shall be adequate, relevant and not excessive) or the fourth principle (personal data shall be kept up-to-date).

Compensation for failure to comply with certain requirements

13.—(1) An individual who suffers damage by reason of any contravention by a data controller of any of the requirements of this Act is entitled to compensation from the data controller for that damage.

(2) An individual who suffers distress by reason of any contravention by a data controller of any of the requirements of this Act is entitled to compensation from the data controller for that distress if—

    (a) the individual also suffers damage by reason of the contravention, or

    (b) the contravention relates to the processing of personal data for the special purposes.

(3) In proceedings brought against a person by virtue of this section it is a defence to prove that he had taken such care as in all the circumstances was reasonably required to comply with the requirement concerned.

GENERAL NOTE

Under the provisions of the 1984 Act, a data subject could only claim, through the courts, for compensation in relation to damages suffered as a result of unauthorised disclosure or inaccuracy of information disclosed. The Act widens the provisions in relation to compensation.

Subs. (1)

This subsection sets out the general principle that a data controller will be liable to compensate an individual who suffers damage as a result of a breach by the data controller of the provisions of the Act. Damage in relation to this section means monetary loss suffered by the individual.

Subs. (2)

This subsection states that an individual is also entitled to compensation for distress suffered as a result of a breach of the provisions of the Act by the data controller if:

    (a) he has also suffered damage due to that breach; or

    (b) the contravention relates to the processing of personal data for special purposes (for example, journalistic, artistic and literary purposes). In this ease, an individual need only prove he has suffered distress and does not have the additional difficulty of proving damage.

This subsection provides a defence to the data controller to an action for compensation where it can prove that it took such care as was in the circumstances reasonable in order to comply with the provisions concerned.

Although compensation is provided for, the Act does not lay down any rules relating to quantification. This will no doubt be a subjective matter, determined by the courts in accordance with the normal rules of quantification in delict (Scotland) and tort (England and Wales).

Rectification, blocking, erasure and destruction

14.—(1) If a court is satisfied on the application of a data subject that personal data of which the applicant is the subject are inaccurate, the court may order the data controller to rectify, block, erase or destroy those data and any other personal data in respect of which he is the data controller and which contain an expression of opinion which appears to the court to be based on the inaccurate data.

(2) Subsection (1) applies whether or not the data accurately record information received or obtained by the data controller from the data subject or a third party but where the data accurately record such information, then—

    (a) if the requirements mentioned in paragraph 7 of Part II of Schedule 1 have been complied with, the court may, instead of making an order under subsection (1), make an order requiring the data to be supplemented by such statement of the true facts relating to the matters dealt with by the data as the court may approve, and

    (b) if all or any of those requirements have not been complied with, the court may, instead of making an order under that subsection, make such order as it thinks fit for securing compliance with those requirements with or without a further order requiring the data to be supplemented by such a statement as is mentioned in paragraph (a).

(3) Where the court—

    (a) makes an order under subsection (1), or

    (b) is satisfied on the application of a data subject that personal data of which he was the data subject and which have been rectified, blocked, erased or destroyed were inaccurate,

it may, where it considers it reasonably practicable, order the data controller to notify third parties to whom the data have been disclosed of the rectification, blocking, erasure or destruction.

(4) If a court is satisfied on the application of a data subject—

    (a) that he has suffered damage by reason of any contravention by a data controller of any of the requirements of this Act in respect of any personal data, in circumstances entitling him to compensation under section 13, and

    (b) that there is a substantial risk of further contravention in respect of those data in such circumstances,

the court may order the rectification, blocking, erasure or destruction of any of those data.

(5) Where the court makes an order under subsection (4) it may, where it considers it reasonably practicable, order the data controller to notify third parties to whom the data have been disclosed of the rectification, blocking, erasure or destruction.

(6) In determining whether it is reasonably practicable to require such notification as is mentioned in subsection (3) or (5) the court shall have regard, in particular, to the number of persons who would have to be notified.

GENERAL NOTE

This section expands on the rights of amendment or erasure granted to individuals under the 1984 Act. The 1984 Act required that inaccurate personal data (or an expression of opinion which appeared to be based on that inaccurate information) be rectified or erased. The Act extends those provisions by allowing an individual the right to apply to a court for the rectification, blocking, erasure or destruction of personal data that are inaccurate, including any personal data that contain an expression of opinion that appears to be based on inaccurate data.

Subs. (2)

This subsection states that the provisions of section 14(1) apply even where the personal data concerned accurately records information provided by a data subject or third party. In these circumstances, and provided that the data controller has taken all reasonable steps to ensure the accuracy of the data, the court may order that the data be supplemented by a statement of true facts. This presents an alternative to the rectification, blocking, erasure or destruction of personal data.

Subss. (3) to (5)

Subsection (3) allows a court that has made an order under section 14(1) to require data controllers to notify any third parties to whom inaccurate data has been disclosed of the blocking, rectification, erasure or destruction of personal data.

Subsections (4) and (5) contain similar provisions. Where a court is satisfied that a data subject has suffered damage as a result of any breach of the Act and that there is a substantial risk of further breaches, the court may:

(a) order rectification, blocking, erasure or destruction of personal data; and
(b) order the data controller to notify any third parties to whom the inaccurate information has been communicated of such action.

Subs. (6)

Under section 14(6), a factor that a court must take into account when deciding whether or not to order the data controller to notify third parties, is the number of third parties involved. This provision suggests that the greater the number of people who require to be notified, the less likely the courts are to make an order.

Jurisdiction and procedure

15.—(1) The jurisdiction conferred by sections 7 to 14 is exercisable by the High Court or a county court or, in Scotland, by the Court of Session or the sheriff.

(2) For the purpose of determining any question whether an applicant under subsection (9) of section 7 is entitled to the information which he seeks (including any question whether any relevant data are exempt from that section by virtue of Part IV) a court may require the information constituting any data processed by or on behalf of the data controller and any information as to the logic involved in any decision-taking as mentioned in section 7(1)(d) to be made available for its own inspection but shall not, pending the determination of that question in the applicant's favour, require the information sought by the applicant to be disclosed to him or his representatives whether by discovery (or, in Scotland, recovery) or otherwise.

GENERAL NOTE

Subs. (1)

Subsection (1) provides that the Court of Session or sheriff courts in Scotland (the High Court or county courts in England) shall have jurisdiction in relation to matters under sections 7 to 14.

Subs. (2)

This subsection allows a court to access any relevant data, as well as any information concerning the logic involved in automatic decision-making, to enable it to determine whether a data subject should be granted access.

PART III

NOTIFICATION BY DATA CONTROLLERS

Preliminary

16.—(1) In this Part "the registrable particulars", in relation to a data controller, means—

(a) his name and address,

(b) if he has nominated a representative for the purposes of this Act, the name and address of the representative,

(c) a description of the personal data being or to be processed by or on behalf of the data controller and of the category or categories of data subject to which they relate,

(d) a description of the purpose or purposes for which the data are being or are to be processed,

(e) a description of any recipient or recipients to whom the data controller intends or may wish to disclose the data,

(f) the names, or a description of, any countries or territories outside the European Economic Area to which the data controller directly or indirectly transfers, or intends or may wish directly or indirectly to transfer, the data, and

(g) in any case where—

(i) personal data are being, or are intended to be, processed in circumstances in which the prohibition in subsection (1) of section 17 is excluded by subsection (2) or (3) of that section, and

(ii) the notification does not extend to those data,

a statement of that fact.

(2) In this Part—

"fees regulations" means regulations made by the Secretary of State under section 18(5) or 19(4) or (7);

"notification regulations" means regulations made by the Secretary of State under the other provisions of this Part;

"prescribed", except where used in relation to fees regulations, means prescribed by notification regulations.

(3) For the purposes of this Part, so far as it relates to the addresses of data controllers—

(a) the address of a registered company is that of its registered office, and

(b) the address of a person (other than a registered company) carrying on a business is that of his principal place of business in the United Kingdom.

GENERAL NOTE

The system of notification replaces the system of registration under the 1984 Act and is intended to be a simpler process. The notification process requires the data controller to give the registrable particulars set out in section 16(1). A notification must also contain a general description of the security measures that data controllers have taken in relation to the personal data they hold. However these security measures will not be included in the register entry.

Under the 1984 Act only those data controllers who had registered could have action taken against them by the Data Protection Commissioner if they were to breach the provisions of the Act. The Information Commissioner is now able, under the new provisions, to enforce the Act against all data controllers whether or not they have taken advantage of the exemptions from the requirement to register in certain circumstances.

The register of notifications is available to the public who can keep track of what data processing activities are being carried on.

The technical details of the notification regime are set out in the notification regulations (Data Protection (Notification and Notification Fees) Regulations 2000 (S.I. 2000 No. 188).

In terms of section 16(2), data controllers are exempt from having to notify any personal data recorded as part of a relevant filing system, forming part of an accessible record or exempt by an order of the Secretary of State. Under section 16(1)(g), a data controller must make a statement that it has exercised its right to this exemption and omitted this processing from the notification. This is so that data subjects are aware that processing is being carried out and can apply under section 24 for a statement of particulars of processing.

Section 16(1)(b) applies where a data controller is established outside the European Economic Area (EEA) but uses equipment based in the United Kingdom for processing personal data (section 5(1)). The data controller in this case must provide the name and address of its representative as part of the notification process.

Subs. (3)

This subsection provides that the address required in terms of section 16(1)(a) for a registered company data controller is its registered office. Sole traders, partnerships and individuals must give the principal place of business in the United Kingdom.

Prohibition on processing without registration

17.—(1) Subject to the following provisions of this section, personal data must not be processed unless an entry in respect of the data controller is included in the register maintained by the Commissioner under section 19 (or is treated by notification regulations made by virtue of section 19(3) as being so included).

(2) Except where the processing is assessable processing for the purposes of section 22, subsection (1) does not apply in relation to personal data consisting of information which falls neither within paragraph (a) of the definition of "data" in section 1(1) nor within paragraph (b) of that definition.

(3) If it appears to the Secretary of State that processing of a particular description is unlikely to prejudice the rights and freedoms of data subjects, notification regulations may provide that, in such cases as may be prescribed, subsection (1) is not to apply in relation to processing of that description.

(4) Subsection (1) does not apply in relation to any processing whose sole purpose is the maintenance of a public register.

GENERAL NOTE

Unless claiming an exemption, a data controller must register under section 18 prior to processing any personal data. It is an offence for a data controller to process data if it has not undergone the notification process (section 21).

Section 17(1) sets out exemptions from the obligation to notify which are:
(a) when data are processed in a relevant filing system (section 1(1)(c)) or when data are contained in accessible records (section 68);
(b) when data are processed for the purpose of safeguarding national security (section 28(1)) or for domestic purposes (section 36); or
(c) when data are processed solely for the maintenance of public registers (section 17(4)).

The Secretary of State may specify further exemptions where he considers that certain types of processing are unlikely to prejudice the rights and freedoms of the individual.

Notification by data controllers

18.—(1) Any data controller who wishes to be included in the register maintained under section 19 shall give a notification to the Commissioner under this section.

(2) A notification under this section must specify in accordance with notification regulations—
(a) the registrable particulars, and
(b) a general description of measures to be taken for the purpose of complying with the seventh data protection principle.

(3) Notification regulations made by virtue of subsection (2) may provide for the determination by the Commissioner, in accordance with any requirements of the regulations, of the form in which the registrable particulars and the description mentioned in subsection (2)(b) are to be specified, including in particular the detail required for the purposes of section 16(1)(c), (d), (e) and (f) and subsection (2)(b).

(4) Notification regulations may make provisions as to the giving of notification—

(a) by partnerships, or

(b) in other cases where two or more persons are the data controllers in respect of any personal data.

(5) The notification must be accompanied by such fee as may be prescribed by fees regulations.

(6) Notification regulations may provide for any fee paid under subsection (5) or section 19(4) to be refunded in prescribed circumstances.

GENERAL NOTE

A data controller must give a notification to the Information Commissioner containing the registrable particulars (section 16(1)) and a general description of the security measures in place to safeguard personal data against unauthorised or unlawful processing, accidental loss, damage or destruction, in accordance with the seventh data protection principle (Schedule 1). A data controller exempt from the obligation to notify may notify voluntarily.

The Data Protection (Notification and Notification Fees) Regulations 2000 (S.I. 2000 No.188) contain rules for notification by partnerships in section 18(4). This clarifies the situation under the 1984 Act that made no special provision for the registration of partnerships. This caused practical problems where partnerships split up or where a small partnership was dissolved and one partner wished to carry on the business as a sole trader. The Notification Regulations state that partnerships are required to give the name of the firm, the principal place of business of the partnership and detail the partners in the partnership. In addition, the Notification Regulations also provide that a partnership is under a duty to notify the Commissioner of any changes in the partnership within 28 days of the change.

Register of notifications

19.—(1) The Commissioner shall—

(a) maintain a register of persons who have given notification under section 18, and

(b) make an entry in the register in pursuance of each notification received by him under that section from a person in respect of whom no entry as data controller was for the time being included in the register.

(2) Each entry in the register shall consist of—

(a) the registrable particulars notified under section 18 or, as the case requires, those particulars as amended in pursuance of section 20(4), and

(b) such other information as the Commissioner may be authorised or required by notification regulations to include in the register.

(3) Notification regulations may make provision as to the time as from which any entry in respect of a data controller is to be treated for the purposes of section 17 as having been made in the register.

'(4) No entry shall be retained in the register for more than the relevant time except on payment of such fee as may be prescribed by fees regulations.

(5) In subsection (4) "the relevant time" means twelve months or such other period as may be prescribed by notification regulations; and different periods may be prescribed in relation to different cases.

(6) The Commissioner—

(a) shall provide facilities for making the information contained in the entries in the register available for inspection (in visible and legible form) by members of the public at all reasonable hours and free of charge, and

(b) may provide such other facilities for making the information contained in those entries available to the public free of charge as he considers appropriate.

(7) The Commissioner shall, on payment of such fee, if any, as may be prescribed by fees regulations, supply any member of the public with a duly certified copy in writing of the particulars contained in any entry made in the register.

NOTE

[1]In relation to any entry in respect of a person which is for the time being included in the register under para. 2(6) of Sched. 14 to the Data Protection Act 1998 as set out in reg. 15 to the Data Protection (Notification and Notification Fees) Regulations 2000 (S.I. 2000 No. 188):

"(4) No entry shall be retained in the register after—

(a) the end of the registration period, or

(b) 24th October 2001, or

(c) the date on which the data controller gives a notification under section 18 of the Act, whichever occurs first.

(5) In subsection (4) "the registration period" has the same meaning as in paragraph 2(2) of Schedule 14."

GENERAL NOTE

This section sets out the Information Commissioner's obligation to maintain a register of notifications. The Information Commissioner must state if the entry is a first time entry in the register and ensure that the entry contains the registrable particulars and all other information that is required under the notification regulations.

Section 19(3) contains provision for the Notification Regulations to determine the date of entry in the register. This is necessary so that data controllers have certainty as to the date from which they can start processing personal data. The date of entry in the register is usually deemed to be the date of receipt of the notification by the Information Commissioner, or the date of receipt by the Post Office of the notification, if sent by recorded delivery or registered post. This is subject to the appropriate fee being paid and the relevant information provided in the notification.

An entry made on the register will not remain valid for longer than the "relevant time", which is 12 months. A renewal fee should be paid at the end of the relevant time or the entry will be removed from the register, with a possible two-month period of grace.

The register is available for inspection at the Office of the Information Commissioner and via the web site at www.dataprotection.gov.uk.

Duty to notify changes

20.—(1) For the purpose specified in subsection (2), notification regulations shall include provision imposing on every person in respect of whom an entry as a data controller is for the time being included in the register maintained under section 19 a duty to notify to the Commissioner, in such circumstances and at such time or times and in such form as may be prescribed, such matters relating to the registrable particulars and measures taken as mentioned in section 18(2)(b) as may be prescribed.

(2) The purpose referred to in subsection (1) is that of ensuring, so far as practicable, that at any time—

(a) the entries in the register maintained under section 19 contain current names and addresses and describe the current practice or intentions of the data controller with respect to the processing of personal data, and

(b) the Commissioner is provided with a general description of measures currently being taken as mentioned in section 18(2)(b).

(3) Subsection (3) of section 18 has effect in relation to notification regulations made by virtue of subsection (1) as it has effect in relation to notification regulations made by virtue of subsection (2) of that section.

(4) On receiving any notification under notification regulations made by virtue of subsection (1), the Commissioner shall make such amendments of the relevant entry in the register maintained under section 19 as are necessary to take account of the notification.

GENERAL NOTE
Data controllers are obliged to regularly update their register entries in regard to any changes to their registrable particulars or security measures. This is so that the register contains the correct name and address and describes the current processing being carried out by the data controller. Failure to notify the Information Commissioner of any of these changes is an offence under section 21. The Information Commissioner is obliged to update the entry on behalf of the data controller when notified of any of these changes.

Offences

21.—(1) If section 17(1) is contravened, the data controller is guilty of an offence.

(2) Any person who fails to comply with the duty imposed by notification regulations made by virtue of section 20(1) is guilty of an offence.

(3) It shall be a defence for a person charged with an offence under subsection (2) to show that he exercised all due diligence to comply with the duty.

GENERAL NOTE
Section 21 creates two offences. The first offence is in contravention of section 17(1) where a data controller processes personal data, has not registered such processing and is unable to claim the benefit of an exemption (for example, the processing is required for national security or domestic purposes).
The second offence is in respect of the failure of a data controller to notify the Information Commissioner of any changes to the register required in terms of section 20, for example, a change in its current name, address or security measures. In relation to this second offence, there is a defence under section 21(3) that the data controller exercised all due diligence (section 47(3)). A data controller found guilty of an offence under the Act is liable to a fine, which can be limited if proceedings are raised in a lower court, but could be an unlimited fine if proceedings are raised in the Crown Court in England and Wales or the Court of Session in Scotland.

Preliminary assessment by Commissioner

22.—(1) In this section "assessable processing" means processing which is of a description specified in an order made by the Secretary of State as appearing to him to be particularly likely—

(a) to cause substantial damage or substantial distress to data subjects, or

(b) otherwise significantly to prejudice the rights and freedoms of data subjects.

(2) On receiving notification from any data controller under section 18 or under notification regulations made by virtue of section 20 the Commissioner shall consider—

(a) whether any of the processing to which the notification relates is assessable processing, and

(b) if so, whether the assessable processing is likely to comply with the provisions of this Act.

(3) Subject to subsection (4), the Commissioner shall, within the period of twenty-eight days beginning with the day on which he receives a notification which relates to assessable processing, give a notice to the data controller stating the extent to which the Commissioner is of the opinion that the processing is likely or unlikely to comply with the provisions of this Act.

(4) Before the end of the period referred to in subsection (3) the Commissioner may, by reason of special circumstances, extend that period on one occasion only by notice to the data controller by such further period not exceeding fourteen days as the Commissioner may specify in the notice.

(5) No assessable processing in respect of which a notification has been given to the Commissioner as mentioned in subsection (2) shall be carried on unless either—

(a) the period of twenty-eight days beginning with the day on which the notification is received by the Commissioner (or, in a case falling within subsection (4), that period as extended under that subsection) has elapsed, or

(b) before the end of that period (or that period as so extended) the data controller has received a notice from the Commissioner under subsection (3) in respect of the processing.

(6) Where subsection (5) is contravened, the data controller is guilty of an offence.

(7) The Secretary of State may by order amend subsections (3), (4) and (5) by substituting for the number of days for the time being specified there a different number specified in the order.

GENERAL NOTE

This section defines "assessable processing" as processing which appears to the Secretary of State likely to cause substantial damage or distress to data subjects or otherwise significantly prejudice their rights and freedoms. The requirement is introduced for prior checking by the Information Commissioner before a data controller can process assessable data. This provision seeks to strike a balance between protecting the rights of the individual and limiting the burdens to be placed on a data controller in the carrying on of its business. It is not expected that this will cover a great number of processing activities.

Recital 53 (pre-amble) of the Directive specifies certain types of processing which are likely to fall into the category of assessable processing, in particular operations which exclude individuals from a right, benefit or contract, or which might pose risks as the result of the use of new technologies.

On receiving a notification from a data controller, the Information Commissioner will examine whether or not the data controller carries out any assessable processing and if so, whether the assessable processing is likely to comply with the provisions of the Act. The Information Commissioner has a period of 28 days from the date of notification by the data controller to serve a notice on the data controller stating to what extent the assessable processing is likely or unlikely to comply with the Act. This period of 28 days may be extended only once in special circumstances and then only for a further period of 14 days, as long as notice of this extended period is served on the data controller within the first 28-day period. The effect of this is that data controllers may be required to wait for up to 42 days from their request to be able to process such personal data.

It is an offence to continue with assessable processing within the period after notification and prior to the Information Commissioner serving the notice on the data controller.

It may be difficult for a data controller to know whether the processing it seeks to carry out is assessable processing and, as it is an offence to carry on processing after notification and prior to receiving the Information Commissioner's notice, it would be prudent for a data controller to take specific steps on each occasion to identify whether the processing might fall into this category.

Power to make provision for appointment of data protection supervisors

23.—(1) The Secretary of State may by order—

(a) make provision under which a data controller may appoint a person to act as a data protection supervisor responsible in particular for monitoring in an independent manner the data controller's compliance with the provisions of this Act, and

(b) provide that, in relation to any data controller who has appointed a data protection supervisor in accordance with the provisions of the order and who complies with such conditions as may be specified in the order, the provisions of this Part are to have effect subject to such exemptions or other modifications as may be specified in the order.

(2) An order under this section may—

(a) impose duties on data protection supervisors in relation to the Commissioner, and

(b) confer functions on the Commissioner in relation to data protection supervisors.

GENERAL NOTE

This provision allows the Secretary of State the power to make an order allowing a data controller the power to appoint an independent data protection supervisor. This may replace the need for data controllers to notify, but there is currently discussion questioning the independence and objectivity of the supervisor who is to be appointed by the data controller. The role of the data protection supervisor will require strict definition within any order conferring the power to appoint them. At the time of publication no such order has been made.

Duty of certain data controllers to make certain information available

24.—(1) Subject to subsection (3), where personal data are processed in a case where—

(a) by virtue of subsection (2) or (3) of section 17, subsection (1) of that section does not apply to the processing, and

(b) the data controller has not notified the relevant particulars in respect of that processing under section 18,

the data controller must, within twenty-one days of receiving a written request from any person, make the relevant particulars available to that person in writing free of charge.

(2) In this section "the relevant particulars" means the particulars referred to in paragraphs (a) to (f) of section 16(1).

(3) This section has effect subject to any exemption conferred for the purposes of this section by notification regulations.

(4) Any data controller who fails to comply with the duty imposed by subsection (1) is guilty of an offence.

(5) It shall be a defence for a person charged with an offence under subsection (4) to show that he exercised all due diligence to comply with the duty.

GENERAL NOTE

An important reason for notification is to ensure transparency of processing. A data controller may not notify certain processing of personal data because it benefits from an exemption under the Act. This means that the description of the personal data will not be available to the public for examination. This section therefore ensures that such transparency is maintained, as a data controller is obliged to supply certain information to any person who makes a request in writing. This information includes the registrable particulars that the data controller would have had to supply when registering. The details of security measures are however not necessary in this instance.

The information must be made available at no charge to the data subject within 21 days of receipt of a request. Failure to supply the information constitutes an offence under section 24(4) although it is a defence to show that the data controller exercised all due diligence.

Functions of Commissioner in relation to making of notification regulations

25.—(1) As soon as practicable after the passing of this Act, the Commissioner shall submit to the Secretary of State proposals as to the provisions to be included in the first notification regulations.

(2) The Commissioner shall keep under review the working of notification regulations and may from time to time submit to the Secretary of State proposals as to amendments to be made to the regulations.

(3) The Secretary of State may from time to time require the Commissioner to consider any matter relating to notification regulations and to submit to him proposals as to amendments to be made to the regulations in connection with that matter.

(4) Before making any notification regulations, the Secretary of State shall—

(a) consider any proposals made to him by the Commissioner under subsection (1), (2) or (3), and

(b) consult the Commissioner.

GENERAL NOTE

This section deals with the obligations on the Information Commissioner and the Secretary of State with regard to the making of the notification regulations and any further amendments to those regulations. Both parties are required to consult with each other and co-operate in the implementation of these regulations. The regulations are currently contained in the Data Protection (Notification and Notification Fees) Regulations 2000 (S.I. 2000 No. 188), which came into force on March 1, 2000.

Fees regulations

26.—(1) Fees regulations prescribing fees for the purposes of any provision of this Part may provide for different fees to be payable in different cases.

(2) In making any fees regulations, the Secretary of State shall have regard to the desirability of securing that the fees payable to the Commissioner are sufficient to offset—

(a) the expenses incurred by the Commissioner and the Tribunal in discharging their functions [under this Act][1] and any expenses of the Secretary of State in respect of the Commissioner or the Tribunal so far as attributable to their functions under this Act, and

(b) to the extent that the Secretary of State considers appropriate—

(i) any deficit previously incurred (whether before or after the passing of this Act) in respect of the expenses mentioned in paragraph (a), and

(ii) expenses incurred or to be incurred by the Secretary of State in respect of the inclusion of any officers or staff of the Commissioner in any scheme under section 1 of the Superannuation Act 1972.

NOTE

[1]Words added by the Freedom of Information Act 2000 (c.36), Sched. 2, para. 17(a).

GENERAL NOTE

The Data Protection (Notification and Notification Fees) Regulations 2000 (S.I. 2000 No. 188) determine the fees for first time notification and the renewal of an entry in the register. The fee for the provision of certified copies of register entries when required are set out in the Data Protection (Fees Under Section 19(7)) Regulations 2000 (S.I. 2000 No. 187).

The fees imposed must be sufficient to cover the expenses of the Information Commissioner, the Tribunal and the Secretary of State in the exercise of their functions under the Act. The Secretary of State may also consider any deficits incurred from previous years when determining the level of the fees.

Part IV

Exemptions

Preliminary

27.—(1) References in any of the data protection principles or any provision of Parts II and III to personal data or to the processing of personal data do not include references to data or processing which by virtue of this Part are exempt from that principle or other provision.

(2) In this Part "the subject information provisions" means —

(a) the first data protection principle to the extent to which it requires compliance with paragraph 2 of Part II of Schedule 1, and

(b) section 7.

(3) In this Part "the non-disclosure provisions" means the provisions specified in subsection (4) to the extent to which they are inconsistent with the disclosure in question.

(4) The provisions referred to in subsection (3) are—

(a) the first data protection principle, except to the extent to which it requires compliance with the conditions in Schedules 2 and 3,

(b) the second, third, fourth and fifth data protection principles, and

(c) sections 10 and 14(1) to (3).

(5) Except as provided by this Part, the subject information provisions shall have effect notwithstanding any enactment or rule of law prohibiting or restricting the disclosure, or authorising the withholding, of information.

GENERAL NOTE

Part IV and Schedule 7 (Miscellaneous Exemptions) set out exemptions to the obligations under the Act to comply with the data protection principles. The exemptions have the effect of limiting the rights of data subjects, although there are safeguards in place to ensure the appropriate application of the exemptions. Certain conditions require to be met by the data controller before any exemption can be claimed and these conditions require the data controller to consider each case where an exemption is claimed on a case-by-case basis.

Section 27 is an interpretation section and sets out the two types of provisions from which personal data may be exempted:

(a) the subject information provisions (section 27(2)); and

(b) non-disclosure provisions (section 27(3)).

The meaning of "subject information provisions" is set out in two parts in section 27(2). First, that personal data are only treated as being processed fairly where the data subject has supplied the data to the data controller and the data controller advises the data subject:

(a) of the data controller's identity or the identity of the data controller's representative;

(b) for what purposes the personal data are being processed; and

(c) of any other information that might be required to ensure the processing is fair.

Where the personal data have been obtained from a source other than the data subject, the data controller must allow the data subject access to information such as:

(a) the data controller's identity or the identity of the data controller's representative;

(b) for what purposes the personal data are being processed; and

(c) any other information that might be required to ensure the processing is fair.

The second part of the meaning of "subject information provisions" is that the data subject has the right of access to the personal data. The exemption from the subject information provisions will therefore allow a data controller to withhold information from a data subject.

Subsection (3) sets out the meaning of "non-disclosure provisions". Basically, these provisions are referred to as "non-disclosure" due to the fact that they impose restrictions on the disclosure of personal data. Again the exemptions are only available to the data controller on a case-by-case basis.

The non-disclosure provisions consist of three main provisions:

(1) personal data can only be treated as having been fairly processed if any disclosure of that personal data does not infringe the disclosure restrictions detailed in Schedules 2 and 3;

(2) any disclosure of personal data must be in accordance with the second, third, fourth and fifth data protection principles (that is, the principles relating to the obtaining of personal data, their agreed purposes, adequacy, relevance, accuracy and the length of time for which the data may be held); and

(3) any disclosure of personal data must take into consideration the data subject's rights to object to processing likely to cause damage or distress, to have any inaccurate personal data about him rectified, erased, blocked or destroyed and to notify third parties to whom this inaccurate personal data has been disclosed of the rectification, erasure, blocking or destruction.

National security

28.—(1) Personal data are exempt from any of the provisions of—

(a) the data protection principles,

(b) Parts II, III and V, and

(c) section 55,

if the exemption from that provision is required for the purpose of safeguarding national security.

(2) Subject to subsection (4), a certificate signed by a Minister of the Crown certifying that exemption from all or any of the provisions mentioned in subsection (1) is or at any time was required for the purpose there mentioned in respect of any personal data shall be conclusive evidence of that fact.

(3) A certificate under subsection (2) may identify the personal data to which it applies by means of a general description and may be expressed to have prospective effect.

(4) Any person directly affected by the issuing of a certificate under subsection (2) may appeal to the Tribunal against the certificate.

(5) If on an appeal under subsection (4), the Tribunal finds that, applying the principles applied by the court on an application for judicial review, the Minister did not have reasonable grounds for issuing the certificate, the Tribunal may allow the appeal and quash the certificate.

(6) Where in any proceedings under or by virtue of this Act it is claimed by a data controller that a certificate under subsection (2) which identifies the personal data to which it applies by means of a general description applies to any personal data, any other party to the proceedings may appeal to the Tribunal on the ground that the certificate does not apply to the personal data in question and, subject to any determination under subsection (7), the certificate shall be conclusively presumed so to apply.

(7) On any appeal under subsection (6), the Tribunal may determine that the certificate does not so apply.

(8) A document purporting to be a certificate under subsection (2) shall be received in evidence and deemed to be such a certificate unless the contrary is proved.

(9) A document which purports to be certified by or on behalf of a Minister of the Crown as a true copy of a certificate issued by that Minister under subsection (2) shall in any legal proceedings be evidence (or, in Scotland, sufficient evidence) of that certificate.

(10) The power conferred by subsection (2) on a Minister of the Crown shall not be exercisable except by a Minister who is a member of the Cabinet or by the Attorney General or the Lord Advocate.

(11) No power conferred by any provision of Part V may be exercised in relation to personal data which by virtue of this section are exempt from that provision.

(12) Schedule 6 shall have effect in relation to appeals under subsection (4) or (6) and the proceedings of the Tribunal in respect of any such appeal.

This section deals with the exemption of personal data from certain provisions of the Act on the grounds of safeguarding national security, although "national security" is not defined in the Act. These provisions are all eight data protection principles, Part II (rights of data subjects), Part III (notification), Part V (enforcement), and section 55 (prohibits the unlawful obtaining, disclosure or procurement of personal data). This section provides extremely wide exemptions to a data controller from having to notify processing, from being subject to the enforcement provisions and from the rights of data subjects to access their personal data whenever national security issues can be shown to exist.

The issue of a certificate signed by either a Cabinet Minister, the Attorney General (in England and Wales) or the Lord Advocate (in Scotland) certifying that the exemption applies is conclusive evidence that the exemption is required on grounds of safeguarding national security.

Subsection (3) provides that personal data that are the subject of the certificate may be described in general terms rather than in specific terms. The certificate may also have prospective effect as well as retrospective affect.

Unlike the 1984 Act, the certificate is challengeable and appeal is to the Data Protection Tribunal, although individuals affected by a certificate have a limited right of appeal. The Tribunal may allow an appeal and quash the certificate if it finds that the Minister did not have reasonable grounds to issue the certificate. Anyone who is affected by a data controller's inability to disclose personal data, as a result of a certificate containing a general description of the data it covers, can appeal to the Tribunal on the grounds that the general description of the data in the certificate should not apply to the personal data in question. The Tribunal has the power to decide what personal data are covered by the general description set out in the certificate. The test of reasonableness is strict, as the Tribunal must apply the same principles as a court would apply in an application for judicial review (see *R. v. Ministry of Defence, ex p. Smith* [1996] Q.B. 517). This strict criterion has the effect of limiting the right of appeal to the Tribunal. If the Tribunal considers that the appeal is well grounded, it can quash the certificate and the exemption will no longer apply.

Subss. (8) to (9)
These subsections relate to the authenticity of a certificate. Anyone disputing the fact that a Minister did not sign the certificate in question must prove this is the case.

Subs. (11)
This subsection provides that the Information Commissioner has no powers of enforcement where an exemption under this section has been claimed and a certificate has been obtained.

Crime and taxation

29.—(1) Personal data processed for any of the following purposes—
  (a) the prevention or detection of crime,
  (b) the apprehension or prosecution of offenders, or
  (c) the assessment or collection of any tax or duty or of any imposition of a similar nature,
are exempt from the first data protection principle (except to the extent to which it requires compliance with the conditions in Schedules 2 and 3) and section 7 in any case to the extent to which the application of those provisions to the data would be likely to prejudice any of the matters mentioned in this subsection.

  (2) Personal data which—
  (a) are processed for the purpose of discharging statutory functions, and
  (b) consist of information obtained for such a purpose from a person who had it in his possession for any of the purposes mentioned in subsection (1),
are exempt from the subject information provisions to the same extent as personal data processed for any of the purposes mentioned in that subsection.

  (3) Personal data are exempt from the non-disclosure provisions in any case in which—
  (a) the disclosure is for any of the purposes mentioned in subsection (1), and

(b) the application of those provisions in relation to the disclosure would be likely to prejudice any of the matters mentioned in that subsection.

(4) Personal data in respect of which the data controller is a relevant authority and which—

(a) consist of a classification applied to the data subject as part of a system of risk assessment which is operated by that authority for either of the following purposes—

    (i) the assessment or collection of any tax or duty or any imposition of a similar nature, or

    (ii) the prevention or detection of crime, or apprehension or prosecution of offenders, where the offence concerned involves any unlawful claim for any payment out of, or any unlawful application of, public funds, and

(b) are processed for either of those purposes,

are exempt from section 7 to the extent to which the exemption is required in the interests of the operation of the system.

(5) In subsection (4)—

"public funds" includes funds provided by any Community institution;

"relevant authority" means—

    (a) a government department,

    (b) a local authority, or

    (c) any other authority administering housing benefit or council tax benefit.

GENERAL NOTE

This section deals with the exemption relating to the processing of personal data on the grounds of crime and taxation. There are four categories set out in subsections (1) to (4). Personal data are therefore exempt from the subject information provisions and the non-disclosure provisions when the reason for processing the data is for crime prevention and detection, the apprehension and prosecution of criminals or the assessment or collection of taxes. Section 29 also allows disclosure of personal data to statutory organisations such as the police to enable them to process personal data outwith the subject information provisions. However, the exemption applies to different provisions in different circumstances.

The first exemption under section 29(1) is effectively an exemption from complying with the first data protection principle (that is, that personal data should be processed fairly and lawfully) except to the extent that it is necessary to comply with the conditions set out in Schedules 2 and 3. This includes an exemption from having to advise individuals about the processing of their personal data (usually provided in the form of a data protection notice) under Schedule 1, Part II, paragraph 2. However, the data controller is still required to justify any processing using one of the Schedule 2 conditions. In addition, because data relating to criminal proceedings or sentencing are considered sensitive personal data (section 2), the data controller must also further justify the processing using one of the conditions contained in Schedule 3. Data are not processed fairly or lawfully, irrespective of the application of the exemption, if the purpose of the processing of data falling within one of the paragraphs in section 29(1) cannot be justified under either Schedule 2 or 3.

The second exemption under section 29(1) is an exemption from complying with the access rights of data subjects to their personal data.

The exemptions are only available when compliance with the first data protection principle or section 7 would prejudice the detection or prevention of crime, the prosecution or apprehension of offenders or the assessment or collection of taxes. The data controller must consider the individual circumstances of each case.

"Crime" is not defined in the Act although, as the Act does not differentiate between different degrees of the seriousness of the crime in question, it is assumed that all crime is caught. The exemption will cover not only crime detection and prevention but also investigation, and applies even where a person is suspected of having committed a crime. The suspicion and investigation element of a crime does not have to result in police action being taken for the exemption to apply. The exemption will therefore also be useful to other bodies involved in fraud and crime prevention and detection.

Subs. (2)

This subsection provides that personal data which are processed by a data controller for the purpose of discharging a statutory function and which include information obtained for that purpose are exempt from the subject information provisions. However, the data will only be exempt if it is likely that the application of the subject information provisions may prejudice any of the purposes specified in section 29(1).

Subs. (4)

Under section 29(4), relevant authorities (defined in section 29(5) as any government department, local authorities or other authority administering housing benefit or council tax benefit) can avoid complying with the subject access requirements as they are able to process personal data to assess whether individuals are evading payment of tax or making fraudulent claims for benefits such as social security or housing benefit. The problem of accountability of these government and administrative bodies is perhaps met in part by the codes of practice provided for under section 51(3). This exemption cannot be used as a general exemption as it is restricted and is only available when required for the operation of systems of risk assessment.

Health, education and social work

30.—(1) The Secretary of State may by order exempt from the subject information provisions, or modify those provisions in relation to, personal data consisting of information as to the physical or mental health or condition of the data subject.

(2) The Secretary of State may by order exempt from the subject information provisions, or modify those provisions in relation to—

  (a) personal data in respect of which the data controller is the proprietor of, or a teacher at, a school, and which consist of information relating to persons who are or have been pupils at the school, or

  (b) personal data in respect of which the data controller is an education authority in Scotland, and which consist of information relating to persons who are receiving, or have received, further education provided by the authority.

(3) The Secretary of State may by order exempt from the subject information provisions, or modify those provisions in relation to, personal data of such other descriptions as may be specified in the order, being information—

  (a) processed by government departments or local authorities or by voluntary organisations or other bodies designated by or under the order, and

  (b) appearing to him to be processed in the course of, or for the purposes of, carrying out social work in relation to the data subject or other individuals;

but the Secretary of State shall not under this subsection confer any exemption or make any modification except so far as he considers that the application to the data of those provisions (or of those provisions without modification) would be likely to prejudice the carrying out of social work.

(4) An order under this section may make different provision in relation to data consisting of information of different descriptions.

(5) In this section—

  "education authority" and "further education" have the same meaning as in the Education (Scotland) Act 1980 ("the 1980 Act"), and

  "proprietor"—

    (a) in relation to a school in England or Wales, has the same meaning as in the Education Act 1996,

    (b) in relation to a school in Scotland, means—

      (i) in the case of a self-governing school, the board of management within the meaning of the Self-Governing Schools etc. (Scotland) Act 1989,

     (ii) in the case of an independent school, the proprietor within the meaning of the 1980 Act,

     (iii) in the case of a grant-aided school, the managers within the meaning of the 1980 Act, and

     (iv) in the case of a public school, the education authority within the meaning of the 1980 Act, and

  (c) in relation to a school in Northern Ireland, has the same meaning as in the Education and Libraries (Northern Ireland) Order 1986 and includes, in the case of a controlled school, the Board of Governors of the school.

GENERAL NOTE

Under section 30, the Secretary of State can by order exempt or modify the subject information provisions with respect to personal data relating to a data subject's physical or mental health or condition. Other orders can be made in relation to records relating to school pupils and social work records. On March 1, 2000, three Statutory Instruments came into force in relation to this section:

  (1) The Data Protection (Subject Access Modification) (Health) Order 2000 (S.I. 2000 No. 413).

  (2) The Data Protection (Subject Access Modification) (Education) Order 2000 (S.I. 2000 No. 414).

  (3) The Data Protection (Subject Access Modification) (Social Work) Order 2000 (S.I. 2000 No. 415).

Regulatory activity

31.—(1) Personal data processed for the purposes of discharging functions to which this subsection applies are exempt from the subject information provisions in any case to the extent to which the application of those provisions to the data would be likely to prejudice the proper discharge of those functions.

(2) Subsection (1) applies to any relevant function which is designed—

  (a) for protecting members of the public against—

     (i) financial loss due to dishonesty, malpractice or other seriously improper conduct by, or the unfitness or incompetence of, persons concerned in the provision of banking, insurance, investment or other financial services or in the management of bodies corporate,

     (ii) financial loss due to the conduct of discharged or undischarged bankrupts, or

     (iii) dishonesty, malpractice or other seriously improper conduct by, or the unfitness or incompetence of, persons authorised to carry on any profession or other activity,

  (b) for protecting charities against misconduct or mismanagement (whether by trustees or other persons) in their administration,

  (c) for protecting the property of charities from loss or misapplication,

  (d) for the recovery of the property of charities,

  (e) for securing the health, safety and welfare of persons at work, or

  (f) for protecting persons other than persons at work against risk to health or safety arising out of or in connection with the actions of persons at work.

(3) In subsection (2) "relevant function" means—

  (a) any function conferred on any person by or under any enactment,

  (b) any function of the Crown, a Minister of the Crown or a government department, or

  (c) any other function which is of a public nature and is exercised in the public interest.

(4) Personal data processed for the purpose of discharging any function which—

(a) is conferred by or under any enactment on—
  (i) the Parliamentary Commissioner for Administration,
  (ii) the Commission for Local Administration in England, the Commission for Local Administration in Wales or the Commissioner for Local Administration in Scotland,
  (iii) the Health Service Commissioner for England, the Health Service Commissioner for Wales or the Health Service Commissioner for Scotland,
  (iv) the Welsh Administration Ombudsman,
  (v) the Assembly Ombudsman for Northern Ireland, or
  (vi) the Northern Ireland Commissioner for Complaints, and
(b) is designed for protecting members of the public against—
  (i) maladministration by public bodies,
  (ii) failures in services provided by public bodies, or
  (iii) a failure of a public body to provide a service which it was a function of the body to provide,

are exempt from the subject information provisions in any case to the extent to which the application of those provisions to the data would be likely to prejudice the proper discharge of that function.

(5) Personal data processed for the purpose of discharging any function which—
(a) is conferred by or under any enactment on the Director General of Fair Trading, and
(b) is designed—
  (i) for protecting members of the public against conduct which may adversely affect their interests by persons carrying on a business,
  (ii) for regulating agreements or conduct which have as their object or effect the prevention, restriction or distortion of competition in connection with any commercial activity, or
  (iii) for regulating conduct on the part of one or more undertakings which amounts to the abuse of a dominant position in a market,

are exempt from the subject information provisions in any case to the extent to which the application of those provisions to the data would be likely to prejudice the proper discharge of that function.

GENERAL NOTE

Personal data processed for the purpose of any of the watchdog functions set out in section 31(2) are exempt from the subject information provisions. This is to provide assistance to data controllers carrying out regulatory and investigatory functions in the public interest. Therefore the rights of the data subject to access personal data held by these bodies are balanced against the ability of these bodies to discharge these functions effectively. However, this exemption raises questions of the accountability of these regulatory and investigatory bodies and codes of practice such as those provided for in section 51(3) may prove important in guarding against potential abuses.

The functions listed in section 31(2) are intended to protect members of the public against financial loss due to dishonesty, malpractice, incompetence or other serious improper conduct by corporate bodies, professionals, bankrupts or institutions. Protection for charities against misconduct or mismanagement and for their property is also provided. Functions that protect the health, safety and welfare of persons at work against risk are also covered.

Subs. (3)

This subsection specifies that the only functions that fall within the list set out in section 31(2) are those that are conferred by legislation, a function of the Crown, a Minister of the Crown or a government department, or any function that is exercised in the public interest.

Subs. (4)

This subsection specifies public bodies whose data processing for the purpose of discharging their statutory function may be exempt from the subject information provisions. However, there are conditions imposed before the exemption can be applied. These are:

(a) the personal data must be processed in order to discharge a statutory function;

(b) the statutory function must be designed to protect the public against maladministration and failure in providing services by public bodies; or

(c) there is a likelihood that the application of the subject information provisions might prejudice the statutory body's discharge of their function in a particular case.

Subs. (5)

This subsection allows the Director of Fair Trading to benefit from the subject information provisions exemption in section 31(1). However, the functions must be conferred by legislation and their purpose must fall within one of the paragraphs in subsection (5)(b)(i) to (iii). This is to regulate against anti-competitive behaviour and protect individuals against unfair trading practices and illegal business activities. An exemption can only be claimed on a case-by-case basis where the application of the subject information provisions would be likely to prejudice the proper discharge of a particular function.

Journalism, literature and art

32.—(1) Personal data which are processed only for the special purposes are exempt from any provision to which this subsection relates if—

(a) the processing is undertaken with a view to the publication by any person of any journalistic, literary or artistic material,

(b) the data controller reasonably believes that, having regard in particular to the special importance of the public interest in freedom of expression, publication would be in the public interest, and

(c) the data controller reasonably believes that, in all the circumstances, compliance with that provision is incompatible with the special purposes.

(2) Subsection (1) relates to the provisions of—

(a) the data protection principles except the seventh data protection principle,

(b) section 7,

(c) section 10,

(d) section 12,

(dd) section 12A, and

(e) section 14(1) to (3).

(3) In considering for the purposes of subsection (1)(b) whether the belief of a data controller that publication would be in the public interest was or is a reasonable one, regard may be had to his compliance with any code of practice which—

(a) is relevant to the publication in question, and

(b) is designated by the Secretary of State by order for the purposes of this subsection.

(4) Where at any time ("the relevant time") in any proceedings against a data controller under section 7(9), 10(4), 12(8), [12A(3)]¹ or 14 or by virtue of section 13 the data controller claims, or it appears to the court, that any personal data to which the proceedings relate are being processed—

(a) only for the special purposes, and

(b) with a view to the publication by any person of any journalistic, literary or artistic material which, at the time twenty-four hours immediately before the relevant time, had not previously been published by the data controller,

the court shall stay the proceedings until either of the conditions in subsection (5) is met.

(5) Those conditions are—

(a) that a determination of the Commissioner under section 45 with respect to the data in question takes effect, or

(b) in a case where the proceedings were stayed on the making of a claim, that the claim is withdrawn.

Data Protection Act 1998

(6) For the purposes of this Act "publish", in relation to journalistic, literary or artistic material, means make available to the public or any section of the public.

NOTE

[1]Words inserted by the Data Protection Act 1998 (c.29), Sched. 13, para. 2(b).

GENERAL NOTE

This section provides that personal data that are being processed for one or more of the special purposes set out in section 3 (*i.e.* journalism, literary and artistic purposes) are exempt from the wide-ranging provisions set out in section 32(2).

This section should also be read in conjunction with sections 44 to 48 of the Act and Article 8 (Right to respect for private and family life) and Article 10 (Freedom of expression) of the European Convention of Human Rights, now incorporated into United Kingdom law by the Human Rights Act 1998.

The competing interest of the argument for freedom of expression and adequate data protection has been an issue for many years. The fear by journalists and the media that their right and ability to collect and process personal data for news and articles would be severely harmed by the Data Protection regime has been addressed since the 1984 Act. Section 32 attempts to strike a balance between the individual's right to privacy and the freedom of the press.

There are three conditions set out in section 32(1) that must be satisfied before an exemption will apply. The first condition set out in paragraph (a) is that any person must process personal data with a view to the publication of any journalistic, literary or artistic material. The second condition under paragraph (b) is that the data controller must reasonably believe that publication is in the public interest. The data controller is directed to consider the importance of freedom of expression when determining whether the publication is in the public interest. Data controllers must take into account any relevant code of practice when determining whether their belief of processing being in the interest of the public is reasonable. The third condition set out in paragraph (c) is that the data controller must believe that compliance with a particular provision is incompatible with the special purposes.

If the conditions under section 32(1) are satisfied, the processing of personal data will be exempt from the provisions set out in section 32(2). These exempt data controllers from having to comply with certain rights of data subjects under Part II of the Act and from the data protection principles (except the seventh principle that requires technical and organisational measures to be taken to safeguard personal data). A data controller will be exempt from having to give information to data subjects about its processing under paragraph 2, Part II of Schedule 1 and from having to justify that processing under Schedule 2 (if personal data), and Schedule 3 (if sensitive personal data).

Other provisions from which the data controller is exempt are:
(a) data subjects' right of access to their personal data under section 7;
(b) their right to prevent processing likely to cause damage or distress under section 10;
(c) their right in relation to automated decision-making under section 12; and
(d) their right to apply to a court for rectification, blocking, erasure and destruction of personal data under section 14.

In determining whether the belief that the publication would be in the public interest is reasonable, a data controller must consider compliance with any relevant codes of practice that have been designated by an order of the Secretary of State. The Data Protection (Designated Codes of Practice) (No.2) Order 2000 lists the codes of practice that have been designated for the purposes of section 32(3). So far, these are:
(a) the code published by the Broadcasting Standards Commission;
(b) the code published by the Independent Television Commission;
(c) the Code of Practice published by the Press Complaints Commission;
(d) the Producers' Guidelines published by the British Broadcasting Corporation; and
(e) the code published by the Radio Authority.

Subss. (4) and (5)

These subsections empower courts to stay (*i.e.* put on hold) proceedings against data controllers under sections 7(9), 10(4), 12(8), 13 or 14 if it appears to the court, or it is claimed by the data controller, that the processing is for any of the special purposes. This is to prevent courts granting "gagging orders" which would restrain the freedom of the Press and freedom of expression. This section will therefore not apply if the data controller has already published the material.

Research, history and statistics

33.—(1) In this section—

"research purposes" includes statistical or historical purposes;

"the relevant conditions", in relation to any processing of personal data, means the conditions—

    (a) that the data are not processed to support measures or decisions with respect to particular individuals, and

    (b) that the data are not processed in such a way that substantial damage or substantial distress is, or is likely to be, caused to any data subject.

(2) For the purposes of the second data protection principle, the further processing of personal data only for research purposes in compliance with the relevant conditions is not to be regarded as incompatible with the purposes for which they were obtained.

(3) Personal data which are processed only for research purposes in compliance with the relevant conditions may, notwithstanding the fifth data protection principle, be kept indefinitely.

(4) Personal data which are processed only for research purposes are exempt from section 7 if—

    (a) they are processed in compliance with the relevant conditions, and

    (b) the results of the research or any resulting statistics are not made available in a form which identifies data subjects or any of them.

(5) For the purposes of subsections (2) to (4) personal data are not to be treated as processed otherwise than for research purposes merely because the data are disclosed—

    (a) to any person, for research purposes only;

    (b) to the data subject or a person acting on his behalf,

    (c) at the request, or with the consent, of the data subject or a person acting on his behalf, or

    (d) in circumstances in which the person making the disclosure has reasonable grounds for believing that the disclosure falls within paragraph (a), (b) or (c).

GENERAL NOTE

Personal data that are used for research purposes, including statistical and historical purposes, are exempt from certain of the data protection rules. "Research" is not defined and is therefore likely to apply to any kind of research including market research and scientific research, provided that the purpose of the research is:

    (a) not targeted at specific individuals; and

    (b) unlikely to cause substantial damage or distress to the data subject.

If the above conditions apply, the personal data are exempt from the second and the fifth data protection principles, and in some circumstances from section 7.

The exemption from the second principle allows personal data to be processed for purposes other than those for which they were obtained, as long as the data were originally obtained for one or more specified lawful purposes. The exemption from the fifth data protection principle means that data can be kept indefinitely. The exemption from section 7 means that, when data that are processed for research purposes and the results do not identify the data subject, the data subject is not entitled to exercise his right of access to his personal data. If the results do identify an individual the data controller will lose the benefit of the exemption.

Subs. (5)

This subsection ensures that the research exemption is not lost if a disclosure is made for research purposes to any person set out in paragraphs (a) to (d). A data controller may still voluntarily allow a data subject access to his personal records and will not lose the benefit of the exemption.

Information available to the public by or under enactment

34. Personal data are exempt from—
(a) the subject information provisions,
(b) the fourth data protection principle and [sections 12A and 14(1) to (3)]',
and
(c) the non-disclosure provisions,
if the data consist of information which the data controller is obliged by or under any enactment to make available to the public, whether by publishing it, by making it available for inspection, or otherwise and whether gratuitously or on payment of a fee.

NOTE
'Words substituted by the Data Protection Act 1998 (c.29), Sched. 13, para. 3.

GENERAL NOTE
Personal data, that by statute must be made available to the general public by the data controller, are exempt from the subject access provisions, the non-disclosure provisions, the requirement to keep the data up-to-date and accurate, and the data subject's right to rectification, blocking, destruction or erasure of data which are inaccurate.

An example of where this exemption would apply is where personal data are processed for the purposes of the Electoral Registrar who acts under a statutory obligation to publish the Electoral Role and make it available to the public. However, the exemption would not apply in relation to any further processing of the data by a purchaser of a copy of the electoral role.

An exemption under this section can only be claimed by data controllers who are under a statutory obligation to process and publicise data and only to the extent required by statute. Data that the data controller is not under a statutory obligation to process will not benefit from the exemption.

Disclosures required by law or made in connection with legal proceedings etc.

35.—(1) Personal data are exempt from the non-disclosure provisions where the disclosure is required by or under any enactment, by any rule of law or by the order of a court.

(2) Personal data are exempt from the non-disclosure provisions where the disclosure is necessary—
(a) for the purpose of, or in connection with, any legal proceedings (including prospective legal proceedings), or
(b) for the purpose of obtaining legal advice,
or is otherwise necessary for the purposes of establishing, exercising or defending legal rights.

GENERAL NOTE
This section is straightforward and simply provides that personal data are exempt from the non-disclosure provisions where it is required:
(a) by law;
(b) for any legal proceedings;
(c) to obtain legal advice; or
(d) to protect legal rights.
The non-disclosure provisions will not exempt data controllers from having to justify their processing under one of the grounds in Schedule 2, and if the processing involves sensitive personal data, under Schedule 3. Data controllers also still have to ensure that personal data remains secure, in spite of the exemption under this section.

Domestic purposes

36. Personal data processed by an individual only for the purposes of that individual's personal, family or household affairs (including recreational purposes) are exempt from the data protection principles and the provisions of Parts II and III.

GENERAL NOTE

This section provides an exemption from the data protection principles and the provisions of Part II (the rights of data subjects) and Part III (notification) of the Act where personal data are processed by an individual for the purpose of that individual's personal, family or household affairs (including recreational purposes). These activities are seen to be fairly innocuous and therefore the exemption in this section is extremely wide. An example of such processing might be an invitation list or address book. An individual can still request an assessment of another individual's processing under section 42 if he feels there has been a contravention of the Act. The Information Commissioner's enforcement powers under Part V of the Act have not been excluded

Miscellaneous exemptions

37. Schedule 7 (which confers further miscellaneous exemptions) has effect.

GENERAL NOTE

This section simply gives effect to Schedule 7 that contains further exemptions.

Powers to make further exemptions by order

38.—(1) The Secretary of State may by order exempt from the subject information provisions personal data consisting of information the disclosure of which is prohibited or restricted by or under any enactment if and to the extent that he considers it necessary for the safeguarding of the interests of the data subject or the rights and freedoms of any other individual that the prohibition or restriction ought to prevail over those provisions.

(2) The Secretary of State may by order exempt from the non-disclosure provisions any disclosures of personal data made in circumstances specified in the order, if he considers the exemption is necessary for the safeguarding of the interests of the data subject or the rights and freedoms of any other individual.

GENERAL NOTE

This section confers powers on the Secretary of State to introduce further exemptions or increase the scope of existing exemptions by order when required, to protect the interests of the data subject or the rights and freedoms of another individual.

Section 38(1) applies where there is a conflict between a data subject's right of access to information and other legislation restricting or prohibiting this right of access. The Secretary of State may make an order stating that the conflicting legislation should prevail but only where it is necessary to protect the interests of the data subject or the rights and freedoms of another individual. If there is no order, the subject information provisions will have effect.

See section 67 for the Secretary of State's powers to make orders in general.

Transitional relief

39. Schedule 8 (which confers transitional exemptions) has effect.

GENERAL NOTE

This section gives effect to Schedule 8 that contains transitional exemptions.

PART V

ENFORCEMENT

Enforcement notices

40.—(1) If the Commissioner is satisfied that a data controller has contravened or is contravening any of the data protection principles, the Commissioners may serve him with a notice (in this Act referred to as "an enforcement notice") requiring him, for complying with the principle or principles in question, to do either or both of the following—
  (a) to take within such time as may be specified in the notice, or to refrain from taking after such time as may be so specified, such steps as are so specified, or
  (b) to refrain from processing any personal data, or any personal data of a description specified in the notice, or to refrain from processing them for a purpose so specified or in a manner so specified, after such time as may be so specified.
(2) In deciding whether to serve an enforcement notice, the Commissioner shall consider whether the contravention has caused or is likely to cause any person damage or distress.
(3) An enforcement notice in respect of a contravention of the fourth data protection principle which requires the data controller to rectify, block, erase or destroy any inaccurate data may also require the data controller to rectify, block, erase or destroy any other data held by him and containing an expression of opinion which appears to the Commissioner to be based on the inaccurate data.
(4) An enforcement notice in respect of a contravention of the fourth data protection principle, in the case of data which accurately record information received or obtained by the data controller from the data subject or a third party, may require the data controller either—
  (a) to rectify, block, erase or destroy any inaccurate data and any other data held by him and containing an expression of opinion as mentioned in subsection (3), or
  (b) to take such steps as are specified in the notice for securing compliance with the requirements specified in paragraph 7 of Part II of Schedule 1 and, if the Commissioner thinks fit, for supplementing the data with such statement of the true facts relating to the matters dealt with by the data as the Commissioner may approve.
(5) Where—
  (a) an enforcement notice requires the data controller to rectify, block, erase or destroy any personal data, or
  (b) the Commissioner is satisfied that personal data which have been rectified, blocked, erased or destroyed had been processed in contravention of any of the data protection principles,
an enforcement notice may, if reasonably practicable, require the data controller to notify third parties to whom the data have been disclosed of the rectification, blocking, erasure or destruction; and in determining whether it is reasonably practicable to require such notification regard shall be had, in particular, to the number of persons who would have to be notified.
(6) An enforcement notice must contain—
  (a) a statement of the data protection principle or principles which the Commissioner is satisfied have been or are being contravened and his reasons for reaching that conclusion, and
  (b) particulars of the rights of appeal conferred by section 48.

(7) Subject to subsection (8), an enforcement notice must not require any of the provisions of the notice to be complied with before the end of the period within which an appeal can be brought against the notice and, if such an appeal is brought, the notice need not be complied with pending the determination or withdrawal of the appeal.

(8) If by reason of special circumstances the Commissioner considers that an enforcement notice should be complied with as a matter of urgency he may include in the notice a statement to that effect and a statement of his reasons for reaching that conclusion; and in that event subsection (7) shall not apply but the notice must not require the provisions of the notice to be complied with before the end of the period of seven days beginning with the day on which the notice is served.

(9) Notification regulations (as defined by section 16(2)) may make provision as to the effect of the service of an enforcement notice on any entry in the register maintained under section 19 which relates to the person on whom the notice is served.

(10) This section has effect subject to section 46(1).

GENERAL NOTE

Part V of the Act together with Schedule 9 gives the Information Commissioner powers of enforcement, inspection and entry. Section 40 specifically deals with enforcement notices that are the main instrument for enforcement of the data protection principles with data controllers.

Although enforcement notices existed under the 1984 Act, data controllers no longer require to be registered before the Information Commissioner can take enforcement action against them. In practical terms the Information Commissioner will generally try to resolve infringements informally before taking the formal steps of enforcement under this part of the Act. However, such informal investigations are at the Information Commissioner's discretion.

In order to be satisfied that an infringement has taken place the Information Commissioner will carry out a preliminary investigation. This can be done by serving an information notice on the data controller, or by inspecting the premises of the data controller, or after receiving a written complaint that fully documents the claim of infringement of any of the data protection principles. An enforcement notice can only be served if the Information Commissioner is "satisfied" that an infringement has taken place. The Information Commissioner should also consider whether the request has caused, or is likely to cause, any person damage or distress. However, the Information Commissioner can issue an enforcement notice even although no person has suffered damage or distress as a result of the breach.

An enforcement notice will require a data controller to take, or refrain from taking, certain specified steps and/or to refrain from processing any personal data in any particular way. The enforcement notice may also require the data controller to comply with any data protection principle that the Information Commissioner believes has been, or is being, contravened and the reasons the Information Commissioner has for reaching that conclusion.

The enforcement notice will also specify time limits within which the data controller must comply with the terms of the enforcement notice. As the data controller has a right of appeal in relation to the notice, the time specified for compliance must not be less than the time within which the data controller can appeal against the enforcement notice.

Subss. (3) to (4)

These subsections deal with enforcement notices issued as a result of a contravention of the fourth data protection principle. The fourth data protection principle requires a data controller to keep personal data accurate, and where necessary, up-to-date. A data controller will be required to rectify, block, erase or destroy any inaccurate data, including any expressions of opinion based on inaccurate data.

If a data controller has received personal data from a data subject or from a third party which is inaccurate, and has recorded those inaccurate data accurately, different provisions will apply. The data controller in this case will either have to rectify, erase, block or destroy this data or take reasonable steps to ensure their accuracy, and where the Information Commissioner thinks necessary, add a true statement of the facts to the data in question.

Subs. (5)

The Information Commissioner may, under section 40(5), where reasonably practical, require the data controller to advise third parties to whom the inaccurate data has already been disclosed that an enforcement notice has been issued to rectify, block, erase or destroy the inaccurate data.

This is to prevent third parties continuing to process inaccurate data about the data subject. The Information Commissioner must strike a balance between fairness to the individual and the burden on a data controller where it may not be practical to notify potentially large numbers of third parties.

Subss. (6) and (7)

The right of appeal against an enforcement notice is made to the Data Protection Tribunal under section 48. There is a further right of appeal to the courts on a point of law, but not on a point of fact, under section 49(6). An appeal suspends the effect of an enforcement notice until the matter has been determined (section 40(7)).

Subs. (8)

Under section 40(8), in certain "special circumstances" the Information Commissioner may require a data controller to comply with an enforcement notice as a matter of urgency. The time limit for compliance with an enforcement notice may be reduced to not less than seven days. The Act does not define what is meant by "special circumstances" although these might be where sensitive personal data are being processed and that processing is causing harm to data subjects. This creates an exception to the rule in section 40(7), where the period within which the data controller must comply with an enforcement notice must not be less than the period within which the data controller can bring an appeal.

Subs. (10)

This subsection provides that enforcement notices may not be issued where the processing is for the special purposes unless the procedure set out in section 46 is followed.

Although a breach of the data protection principles in itself is not an offence under the Act, failure to comply with an enforcement notice is an offence (section 47(1)).

Cancellation of enforcement notice

41.—(1) If the Commissioner considers that all or any of the provisions of an enforcement notice need not be complied with in order to ensure compliance with the data protection principle or principles to which it relates, he may cancel or vary the notice by written notice to the person on whom it was served.

(2) A person on whom an enforcement notice has been served may, at any time after the expiry of the period during which an appeal can be brought against that notice, apply in writing to the Commissioner for the cancellation or variation of that notice on the ground that, by reason of a change of circumstances, all or any of the provisions of that notice need not be complied with in order to ensure compliance with the data protection principle or principles to which that notice relates.

GENERAL NOTE

The Information Commissioner may, at her option or on the request of a data controller, vary or cancel an enforcement notice if there has been a genuine change of circumstances. This is a move forwards from the 1984 Act whereby a notice could only be cancelled and could not be varied. It provides a separate route for the data controller to challenge an enforcement notice without going through the appeal process, although an application to vary or cancel an enforcement notice must only be made after the expiry of the time limit for lodging an appeal.

If the request of the data controller to vary or cancel an enforcement notice is refused, the data controller has the right to appeal against that refusal to the Data Protection Tribunal. Although this is a significant right for data controllers, an appeal will only succeed if there is a genuine change of circumstances, rendering the enforcement notice unnecessary.

Request for assessment

42.—(1) A request may be made to the Commissioner by or on behalf of any person who is, or believes himself to be, directly affected by any processing of personal data for an assessment as to whether it is likely or unlikely that the processing has been or is being carried out in compliance with the provisions of this Act.

(2) On receiving a request under this section, the Commissioner shall make an assessment in such manner as appears to him to be appropriate, unless he has not been supplied with such information as he may reasonably require in order to—

(a) satisfy himself as to the identity of the person making the request, and

(b) enable him to identify the processing in question.

(3) The matters to which the Commissioner may have regard in determining in what manner it is appropriate to make an assessment include—

(a) the extent to which the request appears to him to raise a matter of substance,

(b) any undue delay in making the request, and

(c) whether or not the person making the request is entitled to make an application under section 7 in respect of the personal data in question.

(4) Where the Commissioner has received a request under this section he shall notify the person who made the request—

(a) whether he has made an assessment as a result of the request, and

(b) to the extent that he considers appropriate, having regard in particular to any exemption from section 7 applying in relation to the personal data concerned, of any view formed or action taken as a result of the request.

GENERAL NOTE

Data subjects or any other individuals who believe themselves to be directly affected by processing, and who are concerned that the processing contravenes the provisions of the Act, may lodge a request with the Information Commissioner for an assessment to be carried out on that processing.

The Information Commissioner must satisfy herself as to the identity of the individual. In addition, the individual must be able to identify the processing that is alleged to be in contravention of the Act (section 42(2)).

However, the Information Commissioner may make the assessment "in such manner as appears to be appropriate" so there is flexibility in respect of what action is taken. If the Information Commissioner perceives there to be a legitimate concern, the processing will be assessed to determine whether it complies with the provisions of the Act. Several factors, such as whether or not the person would be entitled to have access to the data under section 7, may influence the manner of the assessment (section 42(3)).

The individual should be advised of the assessment and of the outcome, such as whether an enforcement notice is to be issued. A letter informing the individual that the processing does not concern the Information Commissioner can be considered as an assessment.

It is rare that an individual will be directly concerned by processing where his or her personal data are not included in the processing, although parents and guardians and those with powers of attorney may fall into this category. It is likely that the Information Commissioner will impose a strict interpretation on who is "directly concerned" for the purposes of this section, not least because of the administrative strain that would otherwise be involved. The Information Commissioner also has to determine whether the request raises a "matter of substance" and this may also limit the number of assessments likely to be made.

Information notices

43.—(1) If the Commissioner—

(a) has received a request under section 42 in respect of any processing of personal data, or

(b) reasonably requires any information for the purpose of determining whether the data controller has complied or is complying with the data protection principles,

he may serve the data controller with a notice (in this Act referred to as "an information notice") requiring the data controller, within such time as is specified in the notice, to furnish the Commissioner, in such form as may be so specified, with such information relating to the request or to compliance with the principles as is so specified.

(2) An information notice must contain—

(a) in a case falling within subsection (1)(a), a statement that the Commissioner has received a request under section 42 in relation to the specified processing, or

(b) in a case falling within subsection (1)(b), a statement that the Commissioner regards the specified information as relevant for the purpose of determining whether the data controller has complied, or is complying, with the data protection principles and his reasons for regarding it as relevant for that purpose.

(3) An information notice must also contain particulars of the rights of appeal conferred by section 48.

(4) Subject to subsection (5), the time specified in an information notice shall not expire before the end of the period within which an appeal can be brought against the notice and, if such an appeal is brought, the information need not be furnished pending the determination or withdrawal of the appeal.

(5) If by reason of special circumstances the Commissioner considers that the information is required as a matter of urgency, he may include in the notice a statement to that effect and a statement of his reasons for reaching that conclusion; and in that event subsection (4) shall not apply, but the notice shall not require the information to be furnished before the end of the period of seven days beginning with the day on which the notice is served.

(6) A person shall not be required by virtue of this section to furnish the Commissioner with any information in respect of—

(a) any communication between a professional legal adviser and his client in connection with the giving of legal advice to the client with respect to his obligations, liabilities or rights under this Act, or

(b) any communication between a professional legal adviser and his client, or between such an adviser or his client and any other person, made in connection with or in contemplation of proceedings under or arising out of this Act (including proceedings before the Tribunal) and for the purposes of such proceedings.

(7) In subsection (6) references to the client of a professional legal adviser include references to any person representing such a client.

(8) A person shall not be required by virtue of this section to furnish the Commissioner with any information if the furnishing of that information would, by revealing evidence of the commission of any offence other than an offence under this Act, expose him to proceedings for that offence.

(9) The Commissioner may cancel an information notice by written notice to the person on whom it was served.

(10) This section has effect subject to section 46(3).

GENERAL NOTE

The Information Commissioner can serve an information notice on a data controller if a request has been received under section 42 in respect of the processing of any personal data, or the Information Commissioner has reasonable cause to suspect that a data controller is contravening any of the data protection principles.

An information notice requires a data controller to provide specified information to the Information Commissioner within a specified period of time that will be used to determine whether the data controller has contravened the data protection principles. The notice should explain why the Information Commissioner is requesting the information, *i.e.* either because a request for assessment has been made or the information is required to enable the Information Commissioner to determine whether or not a data controller is complying with the data protection principles.

The information notice should also give details of the data controller's right to appeal to the Tribunal. Similar time limits apply as for enforcement notices. The time limit in which a response must be made should not be more than the time limit laid down for the appeal. In cases of urgency, a shorter period may be set but the reasons for the urgency must be set out in the notice, although in any event, the period for compliance with the terms of the information notice must be not less than seven days. The Secretary of State may make rules of procedure that will provide for an appeal against an information notice to be determined by the chairman or deputy chairman of the

Tribunal sitting alone. This should shorten the time its takes for an appeal against an information notice to be heard.

Subss. (6) to (8)

Under subsections (6) to (8), a data controller is not obliged to provide the Information Commissioner with any of the following information:

(a) any correspondence with a professional legal advisor in connection with legal advice relating to obligations, rights or liabilities under the Act;

(b) any correspondence with a professional legal advisor relating to, or in contemplation of, proceedings under the Act; or

(c) any self-incriminating information that may expose the data controller to any proceedings for the commission of any offence (other than an offence under the Act).

Information notices relating to processing under the special purposes may only be served on a data controller once a determination under section 45(1) has been made.

Subs. (9)

This subsection allows for an information notice to be cancelled by the Information Commissioner by writing to the data controller on which the notice was served.

Special information notices

44.—(1) If the Commissioner—

(a) has received a request under section 42 in respect of any processing of personal data, or

(b) has reasonable grounds for suspecting that, in a case in which proceedings have been stayed under section 32, the personal data to which the proceedings relate—

(i) are not being processed only for the special purposes, or

(ii) are not being processed with a view to the publication by any person of any journalistic, literary or artistic material which has not previously been published by the data controller,

he may serve the data controller with a notice (in this Act referred to as a "special information notice") requiring the data controller, within such time as is specified in the notice, to furnish the Commissioner, in such form as may be so specified, with such information as is so specified for the purpose specified in subsection (2).

(2) That purpose is the purpose of ascertaining—

(a) whether the personal data are being processed only for the special purposes, or

(b) whether they are being processed with a view to the publication by any person of any journalistic, literary or artistic material which has not previously been published by the data controller.

(3) A special information notice must contain—

(a) in a case falling within paragraph (a) of subsection (1), a statement that the Commissioner has received a request under section 42 in relation to the specified processing, or

(b) in a case falling within paragraph (b) of that subsection, a statement of the Commissioner's grounds for suspecting that the personal data are not being processed as mentioned in that paragraph.

(4) A special information notice must also contain particulars of the rights of appeal conferred by section 48.

(5) Subject to subsection (6), the time specified in a special information notice shall not expire before the end of the period within which an appeal can be brought against the notice and, if such an appeal is brought, the information need not be furnished pending the determination or withdrawal of the appeal.

(6) If by reason of special circumstances the Commissioner considers that the information is required as a matter of urgency, he may include in the notice a statement to that effect and a statement of his reasons for reaching that conclusion; and in that event subsection (5) shall not apply, but the notice shall

not require the information to be furnished before the end of the period of seven days beginning with the day on which the notice is served.

(7) A person shall not be required by virtue of this section to furnish the Commissioner with any information in respect of—

(a) any communication between a professional legal adviser and his client in connection with the giving of legal advice to the client with respect to his obligations, liabilities or rights under this Act, or

(b) any communication between a professional legal adviser and his client, or between such an adviser or his client and any other person, made in connection with or in contemplation of proceedings under or arising out of this Act (including proceedings before the Tribunal) and for the purposes of such proceedings.

(8) In subsection (7) references to the client of a professional legal adviser include references to any person representing such a client.

(9) A person shall not be required by virtue of this section to furnish the Commissioner with any information if the furnishing of that information would, by revealing evidence of the commission of any offence other than an offence under this Act, expose him to proceedings for that offence.

(10) The Commissioner may cancel a special information notice by written notice to the person on whom it was served.

GENERAL NOTE

This section allows the Information Commissioner the right to collect information relating to a data controller's compliance with the data protection principles where the data controller is processing personal data for journalism, literary and artistic purposes (the special purposes). The Information Commissioner can only serve a special information notice if an assessment request is received under section 42 in respect of any processing of personal data or, where proceedings have been stayed (*i.e.* put on hold) under section 32, and there are reasonable grounds to suspect that the personal data are being processed for purposes other than the special purposes or other than with a view to publication of any journalistic, literary or artistic material. The duration of stay on proceedings under section 32 depends on whether the data controller's claim to be processing for the special purposes in accordance with the Act is justified. The Information Commissioner may not issue a special information notice in any other circumstances.

The data controller is required to provide the Information Commissioner with the information specified on the notice within the time period set out in the notice. A special information notice must also specify the rights of appeal conferred by section 48.

A data controller can appeal the notice to the Tribunal. The time limit within which to bring the appeal will be less than the time limit set for responding to the notice, unless the Information Commissioner believes the matter is urgent, in which case the notice period will be shortened, although will not be less than seven days.

Subss. (7) to (9)

Under subsections (7) to (9), a data controller is not obliged to provide the Information Commissioner with any of the following information:

(a) any correspondence with a professional legal advisor in connection with legal advice relating to obligations, rights or liabilities under the Act;

(b) any correspondence with a professional legal advisor relating to, or in contemplation of, proceedings under the Act; or

(c) any self-incriminating information that may expose the data controller to any proceedings for the commission of any offence (other than an offence under the Act).

The Information Commissioner may cancel a special information notice by written notice to the data controller.

Determination by Commissioner as to the special purposes

45.—(1) Where at any time it appears to the Commissioner (whether as a result of the service of a special information notice or otherwise) that any personal data—

(a) are not being processed only for the special purposes, or

(b) are not being processed with a view to the publication by any person of any journalistic, literary or artistic material which has not previously been published by the data controller,

he may make a determination in writing to that effect.

(2) Notice of the determination shall be given to the data controller; and the notice must contain particulars of the right of appeal conferred by section 48.

(3) A determination under subsection (1) shall not take effect until the end of the period within which an appeal can be brought and, where an appeal is brought, shall not take effect pending the determination or withdrawal of the appeal.

GENERAL NOTE

This section allows the Information Commissioner to make a determination in writing as to whether processing is being carried out solely for the special purposes or other than with a view to a new publication of journalistic, literary or artistic material. The determination does not have to be in response to a request for assessment or a special information notice as it is entirely at the discretion of the Information Commissioner.

If the Information Commissioner determines that the data are not being processed for the special purposes or with a view to new publication of journalistic, literary or artistic material, any proceedings that have been stayed (*i.e.* put on hold) under section 32 will be resumed.

A determination under this section will also allow the Information Commissioner to issue an enforcement notice regarding the processing for the special purposes, provided that the conditions in section 46(1) are also satisfied.

This section also allows the Information Commissioner to serve an information notice on a data controller in terms of section 46(3).

The data controller must be notified of the determination, and the reasons for the determination, in addition to the right of appeal under section 48.

In conjunction with this section, refer to section 32(4)–(5), section 43(10), and sections 46 and 48.

Restriction on enforcement in case of processing for the special purposes

46.—(1) The Commissioner may not at any time serve an enforcement notice on a data controller with respect to the processing of personal data for the special purposes unless—

(a) a determination under section 45(1) with respect to those data has taken effect, and

(b) the court has granted leave for the notice to be served.

(2) The court shall not grant leave for the purposes of subsection (1)(b) unless it is satisfied—

(a) that the Commissioner has reason to suspect a contravention of the data protection principles which is of substantial public importance, and

(b) except where the case is one of urgency, that the data controller has been given notice, in accordance with rules of court, of the application for leave.

(3) The Commissioner may not serve an information notice on a data controller with respect to the processing of personal data for the special purposes unless a determination under section 45(1) with respect to those data has taken effect.

GENERAL NOTE

The Information Commissioner can only use enforcement notices in respect of processing for special purposes in certain circumstances.

Section 46(1) provides that an enforcement notice cannot be served on a data controller unless a determination under section 45(1) has taken effect (*i.e.* that the processing has not been carried out solely for the special purposes). In addition, the court must grant leave for the notice to be served.

The court may only grant leave if it is satisfied that the conditions set out in section 46(2) have been met. The term "substantial public importance" is not defined and it is a matter for the court to determine on a case-by-case basis.

Section 46(3) provides that information notices cannot be served on a data controller unless a determination under section 45(1) has taken effect (*i.e.* that the processing has not been carried out solely for the special purposes). In this case there is no requirement to obtain leave from the court.

Failure to comply with notice

47.—(1) A person who fails to comply with an enforcement notice, an information notice or a special information notice is guilty of an offence.

(2) A person who, in purported compliance with an information notice or a special information notice—

(a) makes a statement which he knows to be false in a material respect, or

(b) recklessly makes a statement which is false in a material respect,

is guilty of an offence.

(3) It is a defence for a person charged with an offence under subsection (1) to prove that he exercised all due diligence to comply with the notice in question.

GENERAL NOTE

A person who fails to comply with an enforcement notice or a special information notice is guilty of an offence. A person can claim that he has exercised all due diligence to comply with the notice. The degree of due diligence required would depend on the individual circumstances of the case.

In terms of section 47(2), it is also an offence if a person provides information in response to an information notice or special information notice that he knows to be false, or recklessly makes a statement that is false. The response in either case must be false in a material respect.

Rights of appeal

48.—(1) A person on whom an enforcement notice, an information notice or a special information notice has been served may appeal to the Tribunal against the notice.

(2) A person on whom an enforcement notice has been served may appeal to the Tribunal against the refusal of an application under section 41(2) for cancellation or variation of the notice.

(3) Where an enforcement notice, an information notice or a special information notice contains a statement by the Commissioner in accordance with section 40(8), 43(5) or 44(6) then, whether or not the person appeals against the notice, he may appeal against—

(a) the Commissioner's decision to include the statement in the notice, or

(b) the effect of the inclusion of the statement as respects any part of the notice.

(4) A data controller in respect of whom a determination has been made under section 45 may appeal to the Tribunal against the determination.

(5) Schedule 6 has effect in relation to appeals under this section and the proceedings of the Tribunal in respect of any such appeal.

GENERAL NOTE

This section sets out the various grounds for appeal to the Tribunal in respect of enforcement notices, information notices or special information notices. In certain circumstances, a data controller can appeal against any of the notices that have been issued by the Information Commissioner under Part V of the Act. Determination of appeals is dealt with in section 49 and prosecutions and penalties are dealt with in section 60.

Determination of appeals

49.—(1) If on an appeal under section 48(1) the Tribunal considers—

(a) that the notice against which the appeal is brought is not in accordance with the law, or

(b) to the extent that the notice involved an exercise of discretion by the Commissioner, that he ought to have exercised his discretion differently,

the Tribunal shall allow the appeal or substitute such other notice or decision as could have been served or made by the Commissioner; and in any other case the Tribunal shall dismiss the appeal.

(2) On such an appeal, the Tribunal may review any determination of fact on which the notice in question was based.

(3) If on an appeal under section 48(2) the Tribunal considers that the enforcement notice ought to be cancelled or varied by reason of a change in circumstances, the Tribunal shall cancel or vary the notice.

(4) On an appeal under subsection (3) of section 48 the Tribunal may direct—

(a) that the notice in question shall have effect as if it did not contain any such statement as is mentioned in that subsection, or

(b) that the inclusion of the statement shall not have effect in relation to any part of the notice,

and may make such modifications in the notice as may be required for giving effect to the direction.

(5) On an appeal under section 48(4), the Tribunal may cancel the determination of the Commissioner.

(6) Any party to an appeal to the Tribunal under section 48 may appeal from the decision of the Tribunal on a point of law to the appropriate court; and that court shall be—

(a) the High Court of Justice in England if the address of the person who was the appellant before the Tribunal is in England or Wales,

(b) the Court of Session if that address is in Scotland, and

(c) the High Court of Justice in Northern Ireland if that address is in Northern Ireland.

(7) For the purposes of subsection (6)—

(a) the address of a registered company is that of its registered office, and

(b) the address of a person (other than a registered company) carrying on a business is that of his principal place of business in the United Kingdom.

GENERAL NOTE

On appeal, the Tribunal has the power not only to uphold or dismiss appeals but also to do the following:

(a) cancel or change a decision or notice made by the Information Commissioner on the grounds of unlawfulness, abuse of discretion, or mistake of fact;

(b) cancel or change an enforcement notice on the grounds of change of circumstances;

(c) order that a statement by the Information Commissioner regarding the requirement for urgency in compliance with all or part of a notice may be disregarded, or alternatively order that it does not impact on any part or all of the notice; or

(d) cancel a determination made under section 45 against a data controller.

It should be noted that appeals to the courts from the Tribunal can only be made on points of law and not on points of fact.

Powers of entry and inspection

50. Schedule 9 (powers of entry and inspection) has effect.

General duties of Commissioner

51.—(1) It shall be the duty of the Commissioner to promote the following of good practice by data controllers and, in particular, so to perform his functions under this Act as to promote the observance of the requirements of this Act by data controllers.

(2) The Commissioner shall arrange for the dissemination in such form and manner as he considers appropriate of such information as it may appear to him expedient to give to the public about the operation of this Act, about good practice, and about other matters within the scope of his functions under this Act, and may give advice to any person as to any of those matters.

(3) Where—

(a) the Secretary of State so directs by order, or

(b) the Commissioner considers it appropriate to do so,

the Commissioner shall, after such consultation with trade associations, data subjects or persons representing data subjects as appears to him to be appropriate, prepare and disseminate to such persons as he considers appropriate codes of practice for guidance as to good practice.

(4) The Commissioner shall also—

(a) Where he considers it appropriate to do so, encourage trade associations to prepare, and to disseminate to their members, such codes of practice, and

(b) where any trade association submits a code of practice to him for his consideration, consider the code and, after such consultation with data subjects or persons representing data subjects as appears to him to be appropriate, notify the trade association whether in his opinion the code promotes the following of good practice.

(5) An order under subsection (3) shall describe the personal data or processing to which the code of practice is to relate, and may also describe the persons or classes of persons to whom it is to relate.

(6) The Commissioner shall arrange for the dissemination in such form and manner as he considers appropriate of—

(a) any Community finding as defined by paragraph 15(2) of Part II of Schedule 1,

(b) any decision of the European Commission, under the procedure provided for in Article 31(2) of the Data Protection Directive, which is made for the purposes of Article 26(3) or (4) of the Directive, and

(c) such other information as it may appear to him to be expedient to give to data controllers in relation to any personal data about the protection of the rights and freedoms of data subjects in relation to the processing of personal data in countries and territories outside the European Economic Area.

(7) The Commissioner may, with the consent of the data controller, assess any processing of personal data for the following of good practice and shall inform the data controller of the results of the assessment.

(8) The Commissioner may charge such sums as he may with the consent of the Secretary of State determine for any services provided by the Commissioner by virtue of this Part.

(9) In this section—

"good practice" means such practice in the processing of personal data as appears to the Commissioner to be desirable having regard to the interests of data subjects and others, and includes (but is not limited to) compliance with the requirements of this Act;

"trade association" includes any body representing data controllers.

GENERAL NOTE

The Information Commissioner's duties are to promote good practice and to promote the observance of the data protection principles by data controllers.

Good practice is defined in section 51(9) and appears to allow the Information Commissioner complete discretion as to the issuing and consideration of codes of practice, having regard to the interests of data subjects and any other third parties she may wish to consider.

Subs. (2)

Under section 51(2), the Information Commissioner has general duties to disseminate material to the public that she considers appropriate about the operation of the Act, good practice and any other matters within the scope of her functions. She may also give advice to any person on those matters. The material can be in such form and manner as the Information Commissioner considers appropriate. Examples include the Internet publicity campaign and the information service run by the Information Commissioner.

Subs. (3)

This subsection gives power to the Information Commissioner to issue codes of practice either on her own initiative, where she considers it appropriate to do so, or in response to a direction by the Secretary of State. In either case, the Information Commissioner is obliged to carry out a consultation process with trade associations (which definition includes any body representing data controllers such as the Direct Marketing Association), data subjects or persons representing data subjects (which could also include interest groups).

Subs. (4)

Section 51(4)(a) requires the Information Commissioner to encourage trade associations to develop codes of practice and to disseminate them to their members. The section expressly states that this duty applies only where the Information Commissioner considers it appropriate to do so. Use of the word "appropriate" avoids unproductive use of the Information Commissioner's time and resources by ensuring that she is not required in all circumstances to encourage the promotion of codes. In addition, the Information Commissioner has an obligation to consider and comment upon codes of practice that are proposed to her by trade unions. After consultation with data subjects or any appropriate person representing data subjects, the Information Commissioner must notify the trade union as to whether the proposed code promotes the following of good practice.

Subs. (6)

Subsection (6) should be read in conjunction with the eighth data protection principle (Schedule 1, Part II, para. 13, and Schedule 4) relating to the transfer of data outside the EEA (which consists of 15 EU Member States together with Iceland, Liechtenstein and Norway). The Information Commissioner must arrange for the following to be made widely available:

(a) any European community finding;

(b) any decision by the European Commission; and

(c) any other information the Information Commissioner may think necessary to give data controllers in relation to the processing of personal data in countries outside the European Economic Area (EEA).

The Information Commissioner may also charge for any services provided under this Part VI and such charges are to be determined by the Secretary of State.

Reports and codes of practice to be laid before Parliament

52.—(1) The Commissioner shall lay annually before each House of Parliament a general report on the exercise of his functions under this Act.

(2) The Commissioner may from time to time lay before each House of Parliament such other reports with respect to those functions as he thinks fit.

(3) The Commissioner shall lay before each House of Parliament any code of practice prepared under section 51(3) for complying with a direction of the

Secretary of State, unless the code is included in any report laid under subsection (1) or (2).

GENERAL NOTE

Subs. (1)

This subsection places an obligation on the Information Commissioner to lay before each House of Parliament each year a general report on the exercise of her functions under the Act, although the Information Commissioner was under this obligation in the 1984 Act.

Subs. (2)

This subsection allows the Information Commissioner to lay before each House any other reports relative to the functions as she thinks fit.

Subs. (3)

This subsection requires the Information Commissioner to lay before each House of Parliament any code of practice which the Secretary of State has directed by order, unless the particular code in question has been reported in the Information Commissioner's annual general report.

Assistance by Commissioner in cases involving processing for the special purposes

53.—(1) An individual who is an actual or prospective party to any proceedings under section 7(9), 10(4), 12(8), [12A(3)]' or 14 or by virtue of section 13 which relate to personal data processed for the special purposes may apply to the Commissioner for assistance in relation to those proceedings.

(2) The Commissioner shall, as soon as reasonably practicable after receiving an application under subsection (1), consider it and decide whether and to what extent to grant it, but he shall not grant the application unless, in his opinion, the case involves a matter of substantial public importance.

(3) If the Commissioner decides to provide assistance, he shall, as soon as reasonably practicable after making the decision, notify the applicant, stating the extent of the assistance to be provided.

(4) If the Commissioner decides not to provide assistance, he shall, as soon as reasonably practicable after making the decision, notify the applicant of his decision and, if he thinks fit, the reasons for it.

(5) In this section—

(a) references to "proceedings" include references to prospective proceedings, and

(b) "applicant", in relation to assistance under this section, means an individual who applies for assistance.

(6) Schedule 10 has effect for supplementing this section.

NOTE

'Words inserted by the Data Protection Act 1998 (c.29), Sched. 13, para. 4.

GENERAL NOTE

Subs. (1)

An individual has a new right under section 53(1) to request assistance from the Information Commissioner where he is party to proceedings which arise in respect of the processing of personal data for special purposes.

Subs. (2)

Under section 53(2), the Information Commissioner has discretion as to whether to grant assistance and if so, to what extent. However, assistance will only be provided where the Information Commissioner considers it to be a case of substantial public importance. It is not clear what is meant by substantial public importance although Parliament suggested that the Information Commissioner might wish to take legal advice to decide whether a particular case is of substantial public importance. This requirement acts as a filter mechanism by ensuring that public money is not spent on cases where there is little chance of success. It also prevents the new power from being used simply as a legal aid provision to help individuals who do not have the money to bring their cases to court.

The purpose of the clause is to ensure that an appropriate balance is obtained between an individual's rights and those of the data controller, by giving an individual who wants to seek a remedy in the courts additional assistance to do so.

International co-operation

54.—(1) The Commissioner—

(a) shall continue to be the designated authority in the United Kingdom for the purposes of Article 13 of the Convention, and

(b) shall be the supervisory authority in the United Kingdom for the purposes of the Data Protection Directive.

(2) The Secretary of State may by order make provision as to the functions to be discharged by the Commissioner as the designated authority in the United Kingdom for the purposes of Article 13 of the Convention.

(3) The Secretary of State may by order make provision as to co-operation by the Commissioner with the European Commission and with supervisory authorities in other EEA States in connection with the performance of their respective duties and, in particular, as to—

(a) the exchange of information with supervisory authorities in other EEA States or with the European Commission, and

(b) the exercise within the United Kingdom at the request of a supervisory authority in another EEA State, in cases excluded by section 5 from the application of the other provisions of this Act, of functions of the Commissioner specified in the order.

(4) The Commissioner shall also carry out any data protection functions which the Secretary of State may by order direct him to carry out for the purpose of enabling Her Majesty's Government in the United Kingdom to give effect to any international obligations of the United Kingdom.

(5) The Commissioner shall, if so directed by the Secretary of State, provide any authority exercising data protection functions under the law of a colony specified in the direction with such assistance in connection with the discharge of those functions as the Secretary of State may direct or approve, on such terms (including terms as to payment) as the Secretary of State may direct or approve.

(6) Where the European Commission makes a decision for the purposes of Article 26(3) or (4) of the Data Protection Directive under the procedure provided for in Article 31(2) of the Directive, the Commissioner shall comply with that decision in exercising his functions under paragraph 9 of Schedule 4 or, as the case may be, paragraph 8 of that Schedule.

(7) The Commissioner shall inform the European Commission and the supervisory authorities in other EEA States—

(a) of any approvals granted for the purposes of paragraph 8 of Schedule 4, and

(b) of any authorisations granted for the purposes of paragraph 9 of that Schedule.

(8) In this section—

"the Convention" means the Convention for the Protection of Individuals with regard to Automatic Processing of Personal Data which was opened for signature on 28th January 1981;

"data protection functions" means functions relating to the protection of individuals with respect to the processing of personal information.

Subss. (1) to (5)

These subsections set out the jurisdictional reach of the Information Commissioner and the extent of co-operation with other European Economic Area (EEA) States.

Subsection (1) provides that the Information Commissioner shall continue to be the designated authority in the United Kingdom for the purposes of Article 13 of the Convention (http://conventions.coe.int). This Article states that each party to the Convention shall designate one or more authorities who shall at the request of another party to the Convention (1) provide information on its law and administrative practices in the field of data protection; and (2) take, in conformity with its domestic law and for the sole purpose of protection of privacy, all appropriate measures for furnishing factual information relating to specific automatic processing carried out in its territory with the exception of personal data being processed.

Subsection (1) also provides that the Information Commissioner shall act as the supervisory authority in the United Kingdom for the purposes of the Data Protection Directive (http://www.europa.eu.int).

Subss. (6) to (8)

The remaining subsections deal with the transfer of personal data to third countries. They provide that the Information Commissioner must comply with any decision made by the European Commission that a third country does not have an adequate level of protection when exercising her functions under paragraph 8 or 9 of Schedule 4 (that is, cases where the Information Commissioner has authorised the transfer as adequate safeguards have been ensured, or the transfer is made using a model contract that has been approved by the Information Commissioner).

The European Commission can make a decision that a third country does not have an adequate level of security following the procedure under Article 31(2) of the Directive. This provides that a representative of the Commission shall submit a draft of the measures to be taken to a committee composed of representatives of the Member States and chaired by a representative of the Commission. The majority opinion of the committee will determine whether the measures are adopted by the Commission or sent to the Council for decision.

The Information Commissioner is under an obligation to inform the European Commission and the supervisory authorities in the other EEA States of any approvals made under paragraph 8 of Schedule 4 or authorisations made under paragraph 9 of Schedule 4. In accordance with Article 26(3), the Commission or a Member State can object on grounds including the protection of privacy to an authorisation made by a Member State to transfer data to a third country which does not ensure an adequate level of protection.

The Commission may also decide under Article 26(4) that certain contractual conditions offer sufficient safeguards in this situation and Member States must comply with the Commission's decision.

Unlawful obtaining etc. of personal data

Unlawful obtaining etc. of personal data

55.—(1) A person must not knowingly or recklessly, without the consent of the data controller—
   (a) obtain or disclose personal data or the information contained in personal data, or
   (b) procure the disclosure to another person of the information contained in personal data.
(2) Subsection (1) does not apply to a person who shows—
   (a) that the obtaining, disclosing or procuring—
      (i) was necessary for the purpose of preventing or detecting crime, or
      (ii) was required or authorised by or under any enactment, by any rule of law or by the order of a court,
   (b) that he acted in the reasonable belief that he had in law the right to obtain or disclose the data or information or, as the case may be, to procure the disclosure of the information to the other person,

(c) that he acted in the reasonable belief that he would have had the consent of the data controller if the data controller had known of the obtaining, disclosing or procuring and the circumstances of it, or

(d) that in the particular circumstances the obtaining, disclosing or procuring was justified as being in the public interest.

(3) A person who contravenes subsection (1) is guilty of an offence.

(4) A person who sells personal data is guilty of an offence if he has obtained the data in contravention of subsection (1).

(5) A person who offers to sell personal data is guilty of an offence if—

(a) he has obtained the data in contravention of subsection (1), or

(b) he subsequently obtains the data in contravention of that subsection.

(6) For the purposes of subsection (5), an advertisement indicating that personal data are or may be for sale is an offer to sell the data.

(7) Section 1(2) does not apply for the purposes of this section; and for the purposes of subsections (4) to (6), "personal data" includes information extracted from personal data.

(8) References in this section to personal data do not include references to personal data which by virtue of section 28 are exempt from this section.

GENERAL NOTE

Subs. (1)

This subsection prohibits an individual from knowingly or recklessly obtaining, disclosing or procuring the disclosure of information without the consent of the data controller. A person who contravenes this section is guilty of a offence. It was an offence under the 1984 Act to disclose personal data in contravention of the data user's registry entry. However, the offence under section 55 is wider than the offence under the old legislation.

Subs. (2)

This subsection sets out the defences available to an offence under section 55(1). Section 55(1) will not apply where a person can show that the obtaining, disclosing or procuring was necessary for the purpose of prevention or detection of crime, or was authorised under any enactment or legal obligation. It is also a defence if the person involved can show that he acted with the reasonable belief that he had legal authority or that he would have had the consent of the data controller. The final available defence is where the individual can show that the obtaining, disclosing, etc. was justified as being in the public interest. The use of the word "justified" limits the extent of the defence and ensures that the test is more than the simple public interest test.

Subss. (4) and (5)

These subsections provide that it is also an offence to sell or offer to sell information obtained in contravention of section 55(1) or information subsequently obtained in contravention of section 55(1).

Subs. (6)

This subsection provides that any advertisement indicating that personal data are or may be for sale should be regarded as an offer to sell for the purposes of section 55(5). The defences available in section 55(2) cannot be relied upon where an individual sells or offers to sell information obtained in contravention of section 55(1).

Records obtained under data subject's right of access

Prohibition of requirement as to production of certain records

56.—(1) A person must not, in connection with—

(a) the recruitment of another person as an employee,

(b) the continued employment of another person, or

(c) any contract for the provision of services to him by another person,

require that other person or a third party to supply him with a relevant record or to produce a relevant record to him.

(2) A person concerned with the provision (for payment or not) of goods, facilities or services to the public or a section of the public must not, as a condition of providing or offering to provide any goods, facilities or services to another person, require that other person or a third party to supply him with a relevant record or to produce a relevant record to him.

(3) Subsections (1) and (2) do not apply to a person who shows—

(a) that the imposition of the requirement was required or authorised by or under any enactment, by any rule of law or by the order of a court, or

(b) that in the particular circumstances the imposition of the requirement was justified as being in the public interest.

(4) Having regard to the provisions of Part V of the Police Act 1997 (certificates of criminal records etc.), the imposition of the requirement referred to in subsection (1) or (2) is not to be regarded as being justified as being in the public interest on the ground that it would assist in the prevention or detection of crime.

(5) A person who contravenes subsection (1) or (2) is guilty of an offence.

(6) In this section "a relevant record" means any record which—

(a) has been or is to be obtained by a data subject from any data controller specified in the first column of the Table below in the exercise of the right conferred by section 7, and

(b) contains information relating to any matter specified in relation to that data controller in the second column,

and includes a copy of such a record or a part of such a record.

TABLE

Data controller	Subject-matter
1. Any of the following persons— (a) a chief officer of police of a police force in England and Wales. (b) a chief constable of a police force in Scotland. (c) the Chief Constable of the Royal Ulster Constabulary. (d) the Director General of the National Criminal Intelligence Service. (e) the Director General of the National Crime Squad.	(a) Convictions. (b) Cautions.
2. The Secretary of State.	(a) Convictions. (b) Cautions. (c) His functions under section 53 of the Children and Young Persons Act 1933, section 205(2) or 208 of the Criminal Procedure (Scotland) Act 1995 or section 73 of the Children and Young Persons Act (Northern Ireland) 1968 in relation to any person sentenced to detention. (d) His functions under the Prison Act 1952, the Prisons (Scotland) Act 1989 or the

	Prison Act (Northern Ireland) 1953 in relation to any person imprisoned or detained.
	(e) His functions under the Social Security Contributions and Benefits Act 1992, the Social Security Administration Act 1992 or the Jobseekers Act 1995.
	(f) His functions under Part V of the Police Act 1997.
3. The Department of Health and Social Services for Northern Ireland.	Its functions under the Social Security Contributions and Benefits (Northern Ireland) Act 1992, the Social Security Administration (Northern Ireland) Act 1992 or the Jobseekers (Northern Ireland) Order 1995.

(7) In the Table in subsection (6)—
"caution" means a caution given to any person in England and Wales or Northern Ireland in respect of an offence which, at the time when the caution is given, is admitted;
"conviction" has the same meaning as in the Rehabilitation of Offenders Act 1974 or the Rehabilitation of Offenders (Northern Ireland) Order 1978.
(8) The Secretary of State may by order amend—
(a) the Table in subsection (6), and
(b) subsection (7).
(9) For the purposes of this section a record which states that a data controller is not processing any personal data relating to a particular matter shall be taken to be a record containing information relating to that matter.
(10) In this section "employee" means an individual who—
(a) works under a contract of employment, as defined by section 230(2) of the Employment Rights Act 1996, or
(b) holds any office,
whether or not he is entitled to remuneration; and "employment" shall be construed accordingly.

GENERAL NOTE
This section introduces a new offence of "enforced subject access".

Subss. (1) and (2)
Under section 56(1) a person must not, in connection with the recruitment, continued employment or contract for services of another person, require that person or a third party to supply him with or produce to him a relevant record. Section 56(2) prohibits a provider of goods or services from providing or offering those goods or services to another in exchange for the supply or production of a relevant record.
"Relevant record" means any record that has been or is to be obtained by a data subject from any data controller listed in the table set out in section 56, which includes chief officers or chief constables of police, the Secretary of State, and the Department of Health and Social Services for Northern Ireland.
This section covers the instance where a data subject is forced by a third party to hand over his data protection subject access record as a condition of being considered for some form of benefit, for example a job. It is particularly designed to deal with circumstances where such information would reveal prior conviction or caution details.

Subs. (3)

This subsection provides that subsections (1) and (2) do not apply where it can be shown that the imposition of the requirement was authorised by law or order of the court, or was justified as being in the public interest.

Subs. (4)

This subsection states that the prevention of, or detection of, a crime is not justified as being in the public interest for the purposes of section 56(3).

The offence of enforced subject access is reliant upon the coming into force of sections 112, 113 and 114 of the Police Act 1997 (section 112 came into force on the July 1, 1999, although sections 113 and 114 are not yet in force at the date of publication). The Police Act 1997 provides for the introduction of three sets of criminal record certificates as a means of creating an alternative route for the supply of conviction information. However, this is unlikely to be of use to an employer as the new criminal conviction certificates will only be made available to the individual in question. The more detailed criminal record certificate may be available to an employer but only if that employer is a registered person. In order to be registered, employers will have to apply for inclusion and satisfy the Secretary of State that they are likely to recruit to one of the jobs or professions excluded from the Rehabilitation of Offenders Act 1974 (for example, accountants, police, prison service workers).

The remaining subsections contain definitions of terms used in the section.

Avoidance of certain contractual terms relating to health records

57.—(1) Any term or condition of a contract is void in so far as it purports to require an individual—
  (a) to supply any other person with a record to which this section applies, or with a copy of such a record or a part of such a record, or
  (b) to produce to any other person such a record, copy or part.
  (2) This section applies to any record which—
  (a) has been or is to be obtained by a data subject in the exercise of the right conferred by section 7, and
  (b) consists of the information contained in any health record as defined by section 68(2).

GENERAL NOTE

Section 57(1) states that any term or condition of a contract which requires an individual to supply or produce a health record, which has or is to be obtained by an individual exercising his right of access to personal data, is void.

A health record is defined in section 68(2) as any record that consists of information relating to the physical or mental health of an individual and has been made by a health professional in connection with the care of that individual.

This clause should not affect such long established procedures, for example, whereby people give their express consent for a life assurance company to access their health records.

Information provided to Commissioner or Tribunal

Disclosure of information

58. No enactment or rule of law prohibiting or restricting the disclosure of information shall preclude a person from furnishing the Commissioner or the Tribunal with any information necessary for the discharge of their functions under this Act [or the Freedom of Information Act 2000][1].

NOTE

[1]Words added by the Freedom of Information Act 2000 (c.36), Sched. 2, para. 18.

To facilitate full disclosure of information, section 58 provides that obligations under the Act to provide the Information Commissioner or Tribunal with information cannot be restricted by any other statute or other rule of law. Information is the information necessary for the discharge of the functions of both the Information Commissioner and the Tribunal under the Act and the Freedom of Information Act 2000 (together known as the "information Acts").

Confidentiality of information

59.—(1) No person who is or has been the Commissioner, a member of the Commissioner's staff or an agent of the Commissioner shall disclose any information which—

(a) has been obtained by, or furnished to, the Commissioner under or for the purposes of the information Acts.

(b) relates to an identified or identifiable individual or business, and

(c) is not at the time of the disclosure, and has not previously been, available to the public from other sources,

unless the disclosure is made with lawful authority.

(2) For the purposes of subsection (1) a disclosure of information is made with lawful authority only if, and to the extent that—

(a) the disclosure is made with the consent of the individual or of the person for the time being carrying on the business,

(b) the information was provided for the purpose of its being made available to the public (in whatever manner) under any provision of the information Acts,

(c) the disclosure is made for the purposes of, and is necessary for, the discharge of—

(i) any functions under the information Acts, or

(ii) any Community obligation,

(d) the disclosure is made for the purposes of any proceedings, whether criminal or civil and whether arising under, or by virtue of, the information Acts or otherwise, or

(e) having regard to the rights and freedoms or legitimate interests of any person, the disclosure is necessary in the public interest.

(3) Any person who knowingly or recklessly discloses information in contravention of subsection (1) is guilty of an offence.

'(4) In this section "the information Acts" means this Act and the Freedom of Information Act 2000.

Note
'Added by the Freedom of Information Act 2000 (c.36), Sched. 2, para. 19(3).

General Note
The principle of confidentiality contained within the Directive (Article 28(7)), which required Member States to "provide that members and staff of the supervisory authority are to be subject to a duty of professional secrecy with regard to confidential information to which they have access", was enacted by the Act. This section has been amended to include the Freedom of Information Act 2000.

Subs. (1)
This subsection places a restriction on the disclosure of information by the Information Commissioner and her staff. It is clear from the wording of this provision that the duty of confidentiality extends after their employment has ended.

The duty of confidentiality extends to all information that:

(a) is obtained by or disclosed to the Information Commissioner under the information Acts;

(b) relates to an identified or identifiable person or business; and

(c) at the time of disclosure is not, and had not previously been, available to the public from another source.

However, such information may be provided where the disclosure is made with lawful authority.

Subs. (2)

This subsection sets out the conditions where a disclosure can be regarded as having been made with lawful authority. These include:

    (a) the disclosure is made with the consent of the person or individual carrying on business;

    (b) the information was provided for the purpose of being made available to the public;

    (c) the disclosure is made for the purposes of and is necessary for the discharge of functions under the information Acts;

    (d) the disclosure is made for the purposes of any civil or criminal proceedings; or

    (e) a disclosure is necessary in the public interest.

Subs. (3)

This subsection provides that a person who knowingly or recklessly discloses information will be guilty of an offence, unless of course one of the limited conditions in this section is met.

General provisions relating to offences

Prosecutions and penalties

60.—(1) No proceedings for an offence under this Act shall be instituted—

    (a) in England or Wales, except by the Commissioner or by or with the consent of the Director of Public Prosecutions;

    (b) in Northern Ireland, except by the Commissioner or by or with the consent of the Director of Public Prosecutions for Northern Ireland.

(2) A person guilty of an offence under any provision of this Act other than paragraph 12 of Schedule 9 is liable—

    (a) on summary conviction, to a fine not exceeding the statutory maximum, or

    (b) on conviction on indictment, to a fine.

(3) A person guilty of an offence under paragraph 12 of Schedule 9 is liable on summary conviction to a fine not exceeding level 5 on the standard scale.

(4) Subject to subsection (5), the court by or before which a person is convicted of—

    (a) an offence under section 21(1), 22(6), 55 or 56,

    (b) an offence under section 21(2) relating to processing which is assessable processing for the purposes of section 22, or

    (c) an offence under section 47(1) relating to an enforcement notice,

may order any document or other material used in connection with the processing of personal data and appearing to the court to be connected with the commission of the offence to be forfeited, destroyed or erased.

(5) The court shall not make an order under subsection (4) in relation to any material where a person (other than the offender) claiming to be the owner of or otherwise interested in the material applies to be heard by the court, unless an opportunity is given to him to show cause why the order should not be made.

GENERAL NOTE

In accordance with section 60(1), only the Information Commissioner or the Director of Public Prosecutions (England and Northern Ireland) can institute criminal proceedings against any person under the Act.

Subs. (2)

This subsection sets out the penalties if a person is found guilty of a offence under the Act. These are a fine not exceeding the statutory maximum on summary conviction or an unlimited fine for conviction on indictment.

Subs. (3)

This subsection sets out a separate penalty for an individual found guilty of an offence under paragraph 12 of Schedule 9 of the Act (that is, anyone who obstructs the execution of a warrant under the Act).

Subs. (4)

This subsection provides that in relation to certain specified offences under this subsection, a court may order the forfeiture, erasure or destruction of specific documents used in connection with the processing of personal data where it appears to the court that they are connected to the committing of the offence. The specified offences include amongst others:

  (a) processing personal data without notification and a register entry;
  (b) obtaining, procuring or disclosing personal data without the consent of the data controller; or
  (c) failing to comply with the provisions of an enforcement notice or a special information notice.

Subs. (5)

However, section 60(5) qualifies the right of the court to order the forfeiture, erasure or destruction of specific documents. Any person claiming to be the owner or otherwise interested in the material (not the offender) may ask the court not to make an order for the personal data to be forfeited, destroyed or erased.

Liability of directors etc.

61.—(1) Where an offence under this Act has been committed by a body corporate and is proved to have been committed with the consent or connivance of or to be attributable to any neglect on the part of any director, manager, secretary or similar officer of the body corporate or any person who was purporting to act in any such capacity, he as well as the body corporate shall be guilty of that offence and be liable to be proceeded against and punished accordingly.

(2) Where the affairs of a body corporate are managed by its members subsection (1) shall apply in relation to the acts and defaults of a member in connection with his functions of management as if he were a director of the body corporate.

(3) Where an offence under this Act has been committed by a Scottish partnership and the contravention in question is proved to have occurred with the consent or connivance of, or to be attributable to any neglect on the part of, a partner, he as well as the partnership shall be guilty of that offence and shall be liable to be proceeded against and punished accordingly.

GENERAL NOTE

Subs. (1)

Subsection (1) provides:

  (a) where an offence under the Act has been committed by a body corporate, and
  (b) it is carried out with the consent or connivance of, or is attributable to neglect on the part of, an officer of the body corporate,

that officer as well as the body corporate will be guilty of an offence. This means that officers of a body corporate may be personally criminally liable for breaches of the Act. In imposing personal liability on individual members of a company, this section reflects the provisions of section 733 of the Companies Act 1985.

The term "body corporate" is defined in the Companies Act 1985 and includes a company incorporated elsewhere than in Great Britain.

Subs. (2)

This subsection applies the provisions of subsection (1) to a situation where the members of a body corporate manage the affairs of the body corporate. Therefore, where a member by his act or default breaches the provisions of the Act, he may be held personally liable as if he was a director of the body corporate.

This subsection mirrors the provisions of subsection (1) in relation to partnerships. It provides that an individual partner may be held liable for certain breaches of the Act in addition to the other partners in the partnership.

Amendments of Consumer Credit Act 1974

Amendments of Consumer Credit Act 1974

62.—(1) In section 158 of the Consumer Credit Act 1974 (duty of agency to disclose filed information)—
  (a) in subsection (1)—
    (i) in paragraph (a) for "individual" there is substituted "partnership or other unincorporated body of persons not consisting entirely of bodies corporate", and
    (ii) for "him" there is substituted "it",
  (b) in subsection (2), for "his" there is substituted "the consumer's", and
  (c) in subsection (3), for "him" there is substituted "the consumer".
(2) In section 159 of that Act (correction of wrong information) for subsection (1) there is substituted—
  "(1) Any individual (the "objector") given—
    (a) information under section 7 of the Data Protection Act 1998 by a credit reference agency, or
    (b) information under section 158,
who considers that an entry in his file is incorrect, and that if it is not corrected he is likely to be prejudiced, may give notice to the agency requiring it either to remove the entry from the file or amend it."
(3) In subsections (2) to (6) of that section—
  (a) for "consumer", wherever occurring, there is substituted "objector", and
  (b) for "Director", wherever occurring, there is substituted "the relevant authority".
(4) After subsection (6) of that section there is inserted—
  "(7) The Data Protection Commissioner may vary or revoke any order made by him under this section.
  (8) In this section "the relevant authority" means—
    (a) where the objector is a partnership or other unincorporated body of persons, the Director, and
    (b) in any other case, the Data Protection Commissioner."
(5) In section 160 of that Act (alternative procedure for business consumers)—
  (a) in subsection (4)—
    (i) for "him" there is substituted "to the consumer", and
    (ii) in paragraphs (a) and (b) for "he" there is substituted "the consumer", and for "his" there is substituted "the consumer's", and
  (b) after subsection (6) there is inserted—
  "(7) In this section "consumer" has the same meaning as in section 158."

General

Application to Crown

63.—(1) This Act binds the Crown.
(2) For the purposes of this Act each government department shall be treated as a person separate from any other government department.

(3) Where the purposes for which and the manner in which any personal data are, or are to be, processed are determined by any person acting on behalf of the Royal Household, the Duchy of Lancaster or the Duchy of Cornwall, the data controller in respect of those data for the purposes of this Act shall be—

(a) in relation to the Royal Household, the Keeper of the Privy Purse,

(b) in relation to the Duchy of Lancaster, such person as the Chancellor of the Duchy appoints, and

(c) in relation to the Duchy of Cornwall, such person as the Duke of Cornwall, or the possessor for the time being of the Duchy of Cornwall, appoints.

(4) Different persons may be appointed under subsection (3)(b) or (c) for different purposes.

(5) Neither a government department nor a person who is a data controller by virtue of subsection (3) shall be liable to prosecution under this Act, but section 55 and paragraph 12 of Schedule 9 shall apply to a person in the service of the Crown as they apply to any other person.

GENERAL NOTE

The Crown must comply with the provisions of the Act. Servants of the Crown may be prosecuted under section 55 for unlawfully obtaining, disclosing or procuring the disclosure of personal data to another person without the consent of the data controller. Under paragraph 12 of Schedule 9, Crown servants may also be prosecuted for selling unlawfully obtained personal data or for obstructing or failing to give assistance in the execution of a warrant.

Subs. (2)

This subsection states that each Government department shall be treated separately from any other Government department. Note that, whilst the Act does not exempt Government departments from the obligations of the Act and therefore requires them to comply with the Act and process in accordance with the data protection principles, Government departments are immune from prosecution for breaches of the Act.

Transmission of notices etc. by electronic or other means

64.—(1) This section applies to—

(a) a notice or request under any provision of Part II,

(b) a notice under subsection (1) of section 24 or particulars made available under that subsection, or

(c) an application under section 41(2),

but does not apply to anything which is required to be served in accordance with rules of court.

(2) The requirement that any notice, request, particulars or application to which this section applies should be in writing is satisfied where the text of the notice, request, particulars or application—

(a) is transmitted by electronic means,

(b) is received in legible form, and

(c) is capable of being used for subsequent reference.

(3) The Secretary of State may by regulations provide that any requirement that any notice, request, particulars or application to which this section applies should be in writing is not to apply in such circumstances as may be prescribed by the regulations.

GENERAL NOTE

This section applies to:

(a) notices or requests under any provision of Part II of the Act, for example a request by an individual for a copy of any data processed by reference to him;

(b) section 24(1) whereby a data subject can request information about personal data which are exempt from the notification process; or

(c) an application under section 41(2) of the Act concerning a notice by an individual to a data controller to require the data controller to cease processing for the purposes of direct marketing.

However, the section does not apply to anything that must be served in accordance with rules of court.

This section provides that the requirement that any notices or requests referred to above should be in writing is satisfied if they:

(a) are transmitted electronically (for example by e-mail);

(b) are received in legible form; and

(c) are capable of being used for subsequent reference.

Subsection (3) allows the Secretary of State to make further regulations in relation to the provisions of this section to revoke the requirement that notices etc. be in writing.

Service of notices by Commissioner

65.—(1) Any notice authorised or required by this Act to be served on or given to any person by the Commissioner may—

    (a) if that person is an individual, be served on him—

        (i) by delivering it to him, or

        (ii) by sending it to him by post addressed to him at his usual or last-known place of residence or business, or

        (iii) by leaving it for him at that place;

    (b) if that person is a body corporate or unincorporate, be served on that body—

        (i) by sending it by post to the proper officer of the body at its principal office, or

        (ii) by addressing it to the proper officer of the body and leaving it at that office;

    (c) if that person is a partnership in Scotland, be served on that partnership—

        (i) by sending it by post to the principal office of the partnership, or

        (ii) by addressing it to that partnership and leaving it at that office.

(2) In subsection (1)(b) "principal office", in relation to a registered company, means its registered office and "proper officer", in relation to any body, means the secretary or other executive officer charged with the conduct of its general affairs.

(3) This section is without prejudice to any other lawful method of serving or giving a notice.

GENERAL NOTE

Subsection (1) sets out the method that must be used by the Information Commissioner for service of notices upon any person. Different provisions apply depending upon whether the person to be served is an individual, a body corporate or a partnership in Scotland.

The meaning of principal office and proper office are defined in subsection (2).

Subsection (3) states that this section is without prejudice to any other lawful method of serving or giving notice. In other words, there may be other methods of serving or giving notices that can be used.

Exercise of rights in Scotland by children

66.—(1) Where a question falls to be determined in Scotland as to the legal capacity of a person under the age of sixteen years to exercise any right conferred by any provision of this Act, that person shall be taken to have that capacity where he has a general understanding of what it means to exercise that right.

(2) Without prejudice to the generality of subsection (1), a person of twelve years of age or more shall be presumed to be of sufficient age and maturity to have such understanding as is mentioned in that subsection.

The Act does not differentiate between adults and children in respect of the subject information provisions and the requirement to obtain and process data fairly and lawfully. Section 66(1) states that a person who is under sixteen but has a general understanding of the rights he is seeking to exercise under the Act has the legal capacity to exercise those rights.

Subsection (2) provides that a person of 12 years of age or more will be presumed to have such an understanding. If a data controller concludes that a child does not meet the requirements of the above subsections, the parent or guardian of that child is entitled to make the request on his behalf.

The position in relation to access by children is different in Scotland than the rest of the United Kingdom. This is why section 66 contains specific provision to the exercise of rights in Scotland by children. In England there is no specific age at which a child may exercise its rights under the Act. In England, if a child has reached what is known as "the age of discretion", he may exercise his rights under the Act on his own behalf. To determine whether the child has reached the age of discretion, the data controller will need to consider whether the child understands the nature of the request. If it is clear that the child does, the data controller must respond to the child's subject information request in accordance with the Act.

Orders, regulations and rules

67.—(1) Any power conferred by this Act on the Secretary of State to make an order, regulations or rules shall be exercisable by statutory instrument.

(2) Any order, regulations or rules made by the Secretary of State under this Act may—

(a) make different provision for different cases, and

(b) make such supplemental, incidental, consequential or transitional provision or savings as the Secretary of State considers appropriate;

and nothing in section 7(11), 19(5), 26(1) or 30(4) limits the generality of paragraph (a).

(3) Before making—

(a) an order under any provision of this Act other than section 75(3),

(b) any regulations under this Act other than notification regulations (as defined by section 16(2)),

the Secretary of State shall consult the Commissioner.

(4) A statutory instrument containing (whether alone or with other provision) an order under—

section 10(2)(b),
section 12(5)(b),
section 22(1),
section 30,
section 32(3),
section 38,
section 56(8),
paragraph 10 of Schedule 3, or
paragraph 4 of Schedule 7,

shall not be made unless a draft of the instrument has been laid before and approved by a resolution of each House of Parliament.

(5) A statutory instrument which contains (whether alone or with other provisions)—

(a) an order under—

section 22(7),
section 23,
section 51(3),
section 54(2), (3) or (4),
paragraph 3, 4 or 14 of Part II of Schedule 1,
paragraph 6 of Schedule 2,
paragraph 2, 7 or 9 of Schedule 3,
paragraph 4 of Schedule 4,

paragraph 6 of Schedule 7,
  (b) regulations under section 7 which—
    (i) prescribe cases for the purposes of subsection (2)(b),
    (ii) are made by virtue of subsection (7), or
    (iii) relate to the definition of "the prescribed period",
  (c) regulations under section 8(1) or 9(3),
  (d) regulations under section 64,
  (e) notification regulations (as defined by section 16(2)), or
  (f) rules under paragraph 7 of Schedule 6,
and which is not subject to the requirement in subsection (4) that a draft of the instrument be laid before and approved by a resolution of each House of Parliament, shall be subject to annulment in pursuance of a resolution of either House of Parliament.
  (6) A statutory instrument which contains only—
  (a) regulations prescribing fees for the purposes of any provision of this Act, or
  (b) regulations under section 7 prescribing fees for the purposes of any other enactment,
shall be laid before Parliament after being made.

GENERAL NOTE

Subss. (1) to (3)
  Subsection (1) allows the Secretary of State to make orders, regulations, etc. by Statutory Instrument. The Secretary of State also has discretion to make any supplemental provisions to the Act he feels necessary.
  The Secretary of State must consult with the Information Commissioner before making:
    (a) an order other than for setting the dates for commencement of the various provisions contained within the Act; or
    (b) any regulations under the Act other than the notification regulations.

Subs. (4)
  This subsection sets out the Statutory Instruments which are subject to a positive resolution by both Houses of Parliament, for example a Statutory Instrument putting into effect an order exempting other categories of personal data from the subject information provisions.

Subs. (5)
  This subsection sets out the Statutory Instruments which do not require a positive resolution by both Houses of Parliament, for example where the Secretary of State orders the Information Commissioner to prepare codes of practice under section 51(3).
  Fees regulations do not require to be approved by Parliament although do require to be laid before Parliament after being made.

Meaning of "accessible record"

  68.—(1) In this Act "accessible record" means—
  (a) a health record as defined by subsection (2),
  (b) an educational record as defined by Schedule 11, or
  (c) an accessible public record as defined by Schedule 12.
  (2) In subsection (1)(a) "health record" means any record which—
  (a) consists of information relating to the physical or mental health or condition of an individual, and
  (b) has been made by or on behalf of a health professional in connection with the care of that individual.

GENERAL NOTE
  Section 68(1) sets out the definition of "accessible records" and includes health records, educational records and accessible public records.

"Health record" is defined in section 68(2) and is limited to those records made by or on behalf of a health professional. "Health professional" is defined in section 69.

Education records are defined in Schedule 11 and include a record processed by a school, a teacher or other relevant persons in respect of pupils.

A more specific definition of accessible public records is provided in Schedule 12 and includes records that are kept by a local authority specified in that Schedule.

Meaning of "health professional"

69.—(1) In this Act "health professional" means any of the following—

(a) a registered medical practitioner,

(b) a registered dentist as defined by section 53(1) of the Dentists Act 1984,

(c) a registered optician as defined by section 36(1) of the Opticians Act 1989,

(d) a registered pharmaceutical chemist as defined by section 24(1) of the Pharmacy Act 1954 or a registered person as defined by Article 2(2) of the Pharmacy (Northern Ireland) Order 1976,

(e) a registered nurse, midwife or health visitor,

(f) a registered osteopath as defined by section 41 of the Osteopaths Act 1993,

(g) a registered chiropractor as defined by section 43 of the Chiropractors Act 1994,

(h) any person who is registered as a member of a profession to which the Professions Supplementary to Medicine Act 1960 for the time being extends,

(i) a clinical psychologist, child psychotherapist or speech therapist,

(j) a music therapist employed by a health service body, and

(k) a scientist employed by such a body as head of a department.

(2) In subsection (1)(a) "registered medical practitioner" includes any person who is provisionally registered under section 15 or 21 of the Medical Act 1983 and is engaged in such employment as is mentioned in subsection (3) of that section.

(3) In subsection (1) "health service body" means—

(a) a Health Authority established under section 8 of the National Health Service Act 1977,

(b) a Special Health Authority established under section 11 of that Act,

¹(bb) a Primary Care Trust established under section 16A of that Act,

(c) a Health Board within the meaning of the National Health Service (Scotland) Act 1978,

(d) a Special Health Board within the meaning of that Act,

(e) the managers of a State Hospital provided under section 102 of that Act,

(f) a National Health Service trust first established under section 5 of the National Health Service and Community Care Act 1990 or section 12A of the National Health Service (Scotland) Act 1978,

(g) a Health and Social Services Board established under Article 16 of the Health and Personal Social Services (Northern Ireland) Order 1972,

(h) a special health and social services agency established under the Health and Personal Social Services (Special Agencies) (Northern Ireland) Order 1990, or

(i) a Health and Social Services trust established under Article 10 of the Health and Personal Social Services (Northern Ireland) Order 1991.

NOTE

¹Added by the Health Act 1999 (Supplementary, Consequential etc. Provisions) Order 2000 (S.I. 2000 No. 90), Sched. 1, para. 33.

This section lists the category of person who may be regarded as a "health professional" for the purposes of the Act. This includes registered medical practitioners, registered dentists and registered opticians.

"Registered medical practitioner" and "health service body" are also defined in this section.

Supplementary definitions

70.—(1) In this Act, unless the context otherwise requires—

"business" includes any trade or profession;

"the Commissioner" means [the Information Commissioner]';

"credit reference agency" has the same meaning as in the Consumer Credit Act 1974;

"the Data Protection Directive" means Directive 95/46/EC on the protection of individuals with regard to the processing of personal data and on the free movement of such data;

"EEA State" means a State which is a contracting party to the Agreement on the European Economic Area signed at Oporto on 2nd May 1992 as adjusted by the Protocol signed at Brussels on 17th March 1993;

"enactment" includes an enactment passed after this Act and any enactment comprised in, or in any instrument made under, an Act of the Scottish Parliament;

"government department" includes a Northern Ireland department and any body or authority exercising statutory functions on behalf of the Crown;

"Minister of the Crown" has the same meaning as in the Ministers of the Crown Act 1975;

"public register" means any register which pursuant to a requirement imposed—

    (a) by or under any enactment, or

    (b) in pursuance of any international agreement,

is open to public inspection or open to inspection by any person having a legitimate interest;

"pupil"—

    (a) in relation to a school in England and Wales, means a registered pupil within the meaning of the Education Act 1996,

    (b) in relation to a school in Scotland, means a pupil within the meaning of the Education (Scotland) Act 1980, and

    (c) in relation to a school in Northern Ireland, means a registered pupil within the meaning of the Education and Libraries (Northern Ireland) Order 1986;

"recipient", in relation to any personal data, means any person to whom the data are disclosed, including any person (such as an employee or agent of the data controller, a data processor or an employee or agent of a data processor) to whom they are disclosed in the course of processing the data for the data controller, but does not include any person to whom disclosure is or may be made as a result of, or with a view to, a particular inquiry by or on behalf of that person made in the exercise of any power conferred by law;

"registered company" means a company registered under the enactments relating to companies for the time being in force in the United Kingdom;

"school"—

    (a) in relation to England and Wales, has the same meaning as in the Education Act 1996,

    (b) in relation to Scotland, has the same meaning as in the Education (Scotland) Act 1980, and

      (c) in relation to Northern Ireland, has the same meaning as in the Education and Libraries (Northern Ireland) Order 1986;

"teacher" includes—

      (a) in Great Britain, head teacher, and

      (b) in Northern Ireland, the principal of a school;

"third party", in relation to personal data, means any person other than—

      (a) the data subject,

      (b) the data controller, or

      (c) any data processor or other person authorised to process data for the data controller or processor;

"the Tribunal" means [the Information Tribunal][2].

(2) For the purposes of this Act data are inaccurate if they are incorrect or misleading as to any matter of fact.

NOTE

[1]Words substituted by the Freedom of Information Act 2000 (c. 36), Sched. 2, para. 14(a).

[2]Words substituted by the Freedom of Information Act 2000 (c.36), Sched. 2, para. 14(b).

GENERAL NOTE

This section contains definitions of numerous terms used in the Act, including "credit reference agency" and "Minister of the Crown".

The Freedom of Information Act 2000 has amended the terms "Data Protection Commissioner" to the "Information Commissioner" and the "Data Protection Tribunal" to the "Information Tribunal".

Subsection (2) states that data are inaccurate if, for the purposes of the Act, they are incorrect or misleading as to any matter of fact. Inaccurate data are referred to in sections 14(1); 14(3)(b); 40(3); 40(4)(a); Schedule 1, Part II, para.7 and Schedule 13, para.1 of the Act.

Index of defined expressions

71. The following Table shows provisions defining or otherwise explaining expressions used in this Act (other than provisions defining or explaining an expression only used in the same section or Schedule)—

accessible record	section 68
address (in Part III)	section 16(3)
business	section 70(1)
the Commissioner	section 70(1)
credit reference agency	section 70(1)
data	section 1(1)
data controller	sections 1(1) and (4) and 63(3)
data processor	section 1(1)
the Data Protection Directive	section 70(1)
data protection principles	section 4 and Schedule 1
data subject	section 1(1)
disclosing (of personal data)	section 1(2)(b)
EEA State	section 70(1)
enactment	section 70(1)
enforcement notice	section 40(1)
fees regulations (in Part III)	section 16(2)
government department	section 70(1)
health professional	section 69
inaccurate (in relation to data)	section 70(2)
information notice	section 43(1)
Minister of the Crown	section 70(1)
the non-disclosure provisions (in Part IV)	section 27(3)

notification regulations (in Part III)	section 16(2)
obtaining (of personal data)	section 1(2)(a)
personal data	section 1(1)
prescribed (in Part III)	section 16(2)
processing (of information or data)	section 1(1) and paragraph 5 of Schedule 8
public register	section 70(1)
publish (in relation to journalistic, literary or artistic material)	section 32(6)
pupil (in relation to a school)	section 70(1)
recipient (in relation to personal data)	section 70(1)
recording (of personal data)	section 1(2)(a)
registered company	section 70(1)
registrable particulars (in Part III)	section 16(1)
relevant filing system	section 1(1)
school	section 70(1)
sensitive personal data	section 2
special information notice	section 44(1)
the special purposes	section 3
the subject information provisions (in Part IV)	section 27(2)
teacher	section 70(1)
third party (in relation to processing of personal data)	section 70(1)
the Tribunal	section 70(1)
using (of personal data)	section 1(2)(b).

Modifications of Act

72. During the period beginning with the commencement of this section and ending with 23rd October 2007, the provisions of this Act shall have effect subject to the modifications set out in Schedule 13.

Transitional provisions and savings

73. Schedule 14 (which contains transitional provisions and savings) has effect.

Minor and consequential amendments and repeals and revocations

74.—(1) Schedule 15 (which contains minor and consequential amendments) has effect.

(2) The enactments and instruments specified in Schedule 16 are repealed or revoked to the extent specified.

Short title, commencement and extent

75.—(1) This Act may be cited as the Data Protection Act 1998.

(2) The following provisions of this Act—

(a) sections 1 to 3,

(b) section 25(1) and (4),

(c) section 26,

(d) sections 67 to 71,

(e) this section,

(f) paragraph 17 of Schedule 5,

(g) Schedule 11,

(h) Schedule 12, and

(i) so much of any other provision of this Act as confers any power to make subordinate legislation,

shall come into force on the day on which this Act is passed.

(3) The remaining provisions of this Act shall come into force on such day as the Secretary of State may by order appoint; and different days may be appointed for different purposes.

(4) The day appointed under subsection (3) for the coming into force of section 56 must not be earlier than the first day on which sections 112, 113 and 115 of the Police Act 1997 (which provide for the issue by the Secretary of State of criminal conviction certificates, criminal record certificates and enhanced criminal record certificates) are all in force.

(5) Subject to subsection (6), this Act extends to Northern Ireland.

(6) Any amendment, repeal or revocation made by Schedule 15 or 16 has the same extent as that of the enactment or instrument to which it relates.

GENERAL NOTE

Section 75(2) lists the provisions of the Act that came into force on the day Royal Assent was received (July 16, 1998). Such provisions include the definitions, sensitive personal data, the special purposes and the Information Commissioner's functions in connection with the notification regulations. Effectively, these were the provisions necessary to enable the subordinate legislation to be made.

The Act came into full force on March 1, 2000 once all the necessary subordinate legislation had been generated.

SCHEDULES

SCHEDULE 1

Section 4(1) and 2

THE DATA PROTECTION PRINCIPLES

PART I

THE PRINCIPLES

1. Personal data shall be processed fairly and lawfully and, in particular, shall not be processed unless—

(a) at least one of the conditions in Schedule 2 is met, and

(b) in the case of sensitive personal data, at least one of the conditions in Schedule 3 is also met.

2. Personal data shall be obtained only for one or more specified and lawful purposes, and shall not be further processed in any manner incompatible with that purpose or those purposes.

3. Personal data shall be adequate, relevant and not excessive in relation to the purpose or purposes for which they are processed.

4. Personal data shall be accurate and, where necessary, kept up to date.

5. Personal data processed for any purpose or purposes shall not be kept for longer than is necessary for that purpose or those purposes.

6. Personal data shall be processed in accordance with the rights of data subjects under this Act.

7. Appropriate technical and organisational measures shall be taken against unauthorised or unlawful processing of personal data and against accidental loss or destruction of, or damage to, personal data.

8. Personal data shall not be transferred to a country or territory outside the European Economic Area unless that country or territory ensures an adequate level of protection for the rights and freedoms of data subjects in relation to the processing of personal data.

Data Protection Act 1998

GENERAL NOTE

Schedule 1 is divided into two parts. The first part contains the eight data protection principles and the second part provides an interpretation of six of the eight principles. The Act does not contain an interpretation of the third and fifth principles as these are considered self-explanatory.

The Principles

The data protection principles are the most fundamental part of the Act, imposing obligations on data controllers, conferring rights on data subjects and setting out the ground rules for the processing of personal data. Section 4(4) imposes a statutory duty on data controllers to comply with the principles, whether or not they have complied with the notification procedure under section 18. However, it should be noted that not all data are subject to the principles and Part IV contains the various exemptions.

The First Principle

The first principle requires that personal data should be processed fairly and lawfully and prohibits the processing of personal data unless it can be justified under at least one of the conditions set out in Schedule 2. If sensitive personal data are being processed, at least one of the conditions under Schedule 3 must also be met. Processing must be fair and lawful. Where processing cannot be justified under one of the conditions in Schedule 2, or where applicable Schedule 3, or where it has not been notified under section 18, it will be deemed unlawful.

The Second Principle

The second principle states that personal data shall be obtained only for one or more specified and lawful purposes, and shall not be further processed in any manner incompatible with that purpose or purposes.

Schedule 1, Part II, paragraph 5 specifies two methods by which personal data may be obtained for "specified and lawful purposes". The first method is by providing a data protection notice as provided for by paragraph 2 of Schedule 1, Part II. The second method is by notification under Part III of the Act (that is, registration).

The Third Principle

The third principle provides that personal data shall be adequate, relevant and not excessive in relation to the purpose or purposes for which they are processed. No interpretation of this provision is given in Part II of Schedule 1 as it is fairly straightforward and self-explanatory. Data controllers should ensure that they do not obtain more information from data subjects than necessary and any irrelevant data should be destroyed. Certain information may be relevant to some data subjects while not relevant to others and it is therefore important that the same level of information is not obtained from all data subjects. When the purpose of the processing is being determined, regard must be given to the purposes notified to the Information Commissioner and also given in any data protection notice provided under paragraph 2 of Schedule 1, Part II.

The Fourth Principle

The fourth principle provides that personal data shall be accurate and, where necessary, kept up to date. Data controllers should not simply rely on personal data being accurate just because a data subject or a third party has provided the personal data. They should take reasonable steps to ensure the accuracy of all data they process. If the data subject has notified the data controller that he considers the data to be inaccurate, the data must indicate that fact. Section 70(2) offers guidance as to the meaning of "inaccurate". It states that data are inaccurate if they are incorrect or misleading as to any matter of fact. Section 14 provides that the court may order the rectification, blocking, erasure or destruction of inaccurate data and of any data that contains an expression of opinion that is based on inaccurate data.

The Fifth Principle

No interpretation is given for the fifth principle. In essence it states that data should be reviewed regularly and should not be kept for longer than is necessary for the purpose or purposes of the processing. The Act gives no guidance as to the length of time data should be kept. Obviously the length of time data should be retained depends on the particular circumstances. In some circumstances there are legal requirements as to the length of time that data should be kept. For example, in cases of personal injury, personal data must be kept for a period of at least three years. In cases involving contractual disputes or VAT records, records must be kept for six years. Data controllers are obliged to regularly check personal data to ensure that they are not retained for longer than necessary.

An exemption from this principle applies in the case of data obtained for research purposes that may be retained indefinitely, subject to compliance with certain conditions (section 33(1)).

The Sixth Principle

The sixth principle states that personal data shall be processed in accordance with the rights of the data subjects under the Act. This principle empowers the Information Commissioner to enforce the rights of data subjects (under Part II of the Act) against data controllers. A contravention of section 7 (subject access), section 10 (the right to prevent processing which might cause damage and distress), section 11 (the right to prevent processing for the purposes of direct marketing) or section 12 (the rights regarding automated decision making) is held to be in contravention of the sixth data protection principle.

The Seventh Principle

The seventh principle states that data controllers are required to concentrate on two particular but related areas of security, technical and organisational measures to safeguard personal data from becoming subjected to either unauthorised or unlawful processing or accidental loss, destruction or damage. Technical measures include passwords, virus scanning software, firewalls, etc. Organisational measures include the physical security of premises, training of staff, and the monitoring of data within the business of the data controller.

The Eighth Principle

The eighth principle is in implementation of Article 25 of the Directive and prohibits the transfer of personal data to countries outwith the European Economic Area (EEA) unless that country has in place an adequate level of protection. To decide whether a country has an adequate level of protection a data controller must consider several factors. The level of protection is not required to be equivalent to the protection offered in the United Kingdom, but it must be adequate.

PART II

INTERPRETATION OF THE PRINCIPLES IN PART I

The first principle

1.—(1) In determining for the purposes of the first principle whether personal data are processed fairly, regard is to be had to the method by which they are obtained, including in particular whether any person from whom they are obtained is deceived or misled as to the purpose or purposes for which they are to be processed.

(2) Subject to paragraph 2, for the purposes of the first principle data are to be treated as obtained fairly if they consist of information obtained from a person who—

(a) is authorised by or under any enactment to supply it, or

(b) is required to supply it by or under any enactment or by any convention or other instrument imposing an international obligation on the United Kingdom.

2.—(1) Subject to paragraph 3, for the purposes of the first principle personal data are not to be treated as processed fairly unless—

(a) in the case of data obtained from the data subject, the data controller ensures so far as practicable that the data subject has, is provided with, or has made readily available to him, the information specified in subparagraph (3), and

(b) in any other case, the data controller ensures so far as practicable that, before the relevant time or as soon as practicable after that time, the data subject has, is provided with, or has made readily available to him, the information specified in sub-paragraph (3).

(2) In sub-paragraph (1)(b) "the relevant time" means—

(a) the time when the data controller first processes the data, or

(b) in a case where at that time disclosure to a third party within a reasonable period is envisaged—

(i) if the data are in fact disclosed to such a person within that period, the time when the data are first disclosed,

(ii) if within that period the data controller becomes, or ought to become, aware that the data are unlikely to be disclosed to such a person within that period, the time when the data controller does become, or ought to become, so aware, or

(iii) in any other case, the end of that period.

(3) The information referred to in sub-paragraph (1) is as follows, namely—

(a) the identity of the data controller,

(b) if he has nominated a representative for the purposes of this Act, the identity of that representative,

(c) the purpose or purposes for which the data are intended to be processed, and

(d) any further information which is necessary, having regard to the specific circumstances in which the data are or are to be processed, to enable processing in respect of the data subject to be fair.

3.—(1) Paragraph 2(1)(b) does not apply where either of the primary conditions in sub-paragraph (2), together with such further conditions as may be prescribed by the Secretary of State by order, are met.

(2) The primary conditions referred to in sub-paragraph (1) are—

(a) that the provision of that information would involve a disproportionate effort, or

(b) that the recording of the information to be contained in the data by, or the disclosure of the data by, the data controller is necessary for compliance with any legal obligation to which the data controller is subject, other than an obligation imposed by contract.

4.—(1) Personal data which contain a general identifier falling within a description prescribed by the Secretary of State by order are not to be treated as processed fairly and lawfully unless they are processed in compliance with any conditions so prescribed in relation to general identifiers of that description.

(2) In sub-paragraph (1) "a general identifier" means any identifier (such as, for example, a number or code used for identification purposes) which—

(a) relates to an individual, and

(b) forms part of a set of similar identifiers which is of general application.

GENERAL NOTE

In determining whether data are being fairly processed it is important to ensure that the methods of obtaining the data are fair and do not mislead or deceive anyone. If the person from whom personal data are obtained is authorised or required by statute to supply the data, such as data obtained from the Land Registry or the electoral register, it is presumed that the personal data have been fairly obtained. However, compliance with paragraph 2 of Schedule 1, Part II is still necessary.

Paragraph 2 of Schedule 1, Part II requires that certain information should be given to data subjects at certain times. This is to ensure that data subjects know who is processing their personal data and why. Personal data will not be considered as being fairly processed unless this information is provided. The required information is set out in paragraph 2(3), and consists of the following:

(a) the identity of the data controller or his representative;

(b) information as to why the data are to be processed; and

(c) any further information necessary to enable the processing of the data to be fair.

The information does not have to be communicated in writing but may be given face to face or by telephone. The information must be given to the data subject at the time of collecting the personal data and not at a later stage. If someone other than the data subject provides personal data about that data subject, then either before the "relevant time" or as soon as possible afterwards, the required information must be supplied to the data subject.

Paragraph 2(2) defines what is meant by "relevant time". In many cases the "relevant time" will be when the data are first obtained. It is suggested that it might be simpler for data controllers to provide the required information to all customers or data subjects at the time where their personal data are sought. However, if the data controller plans to disclose the data to a third party within a reasonable period then different rules apply (see paragraph 2(2)(b)).

Paragraph 3 sets out two exclusions from the requirement to give the information to data subjects whose personal data have been obtained from third parties. These exclusions are in addition to the Part IV exemptions. The exclusions do not apply where the data subject has supplied his personal data, although the exemptions in Part IV may come into force.

The first exclusion applies if supplying the information would involve a "disproportionate effort". In determining if supplying the information would involve a disproportionate effort, a data controller should consider the number of data subjects to whom the information must be supplied, how old the data are, the expense and the ease of providing the information. This should be balanced against the benefit to the data subject, and also if there would be any adverse effects on the data subject if the required information were not provided.

The second exclusion applies if the recording or disclosure of the data by the data controller is necessary for the compliance with a legal obligation to which the data controller is bound, other than an obligation imposed by contract.

The Secretary of State may make an order regulating the use of personal data containing general identifiers, for example numbers or codes relating to individuals such as National Insurance numbers. Under paragraph 4, personal data containing personal identifiers are considered fairly and lawfully processed only if they are processed according to conditions set out in that order.

Schedules

The second principle

5. The purpose or purposes for which personal data are obtained may in particular be specified—

(a) in a notice given for the purposes of paragraph 2 by the data controller to the data subject, or

(b) in a notification given to the Commissioner under Part III of this Act.

6. In determining whether any disclosure of personal data is compatible with the purpose or purposes for which the data were obtained, regard is to be had to the purpose or purposes for which the personal data are intended to be processed by any person to whom they are disclosed.

GENERAL NOTE

Paragraph 5 specifies two methods by which personal data may be obtained for "specified and lawful purposes". The first method is by providing a data protection notice as provided for by paragraph 2 of Schedule 1. The second method is by notification under Part III of the Act (that is, registration).

In circumstances where it is difficult to comply with these methods, either because it would involve disproportionate effort, or because an exemption might apply, a data controller is still obliged to comply with the second principle by some other method. For example, a statement of processing under section 24 could be issued.

The obligation that personal data should not be further processed in any manner incompatible with the purpose for which the data were obtained applies not only to data controllers but also to their representatives, employees, agents, etc. Paragraph 6 ensures that a data controller should exercise control over subsequent processing by third parties to whom the personal data are disclosed. An example of this might be a clause in a contract restricting the processing of data to the purposes for which the data were obtained.

The fourth principle

7. The fourth principle is not to be regarded as being contravened by reason of any inaccuracy in personal data which accurately record information obtained by the data controller from the data subject or a third party in a case where—

(a) having regard to the purpose or purposes for which the data were obtained and further processed, the data controller has taken reasonable steps to ensure the accuracy of the data, and

(b) if the data subject has notified the data controller of the data subject's view that the data are inaccurate, the data indicate that fact.

GENERAL NOTE

Data controllers should not simply rely on personal data being accurate just because a data subject or a third party has provided the personal data. They should take reasonable steps to ensure the accuracy of all data they process. If the data subject has notified the data controller that he considers the data to be inaccurate, the data must indicate that fact. Section 70(2) offers guidance as to the meaning of "inaccurate" as it states that data are inaccurate if they are incorrect or misleading as to any matter of fact. Section 14 provides that the court may order the rectification, blocking, erasure or destruction of inaccurate data and of any data that contains an expression of opinion that is based on inaccurate data.

The processing of inaccurate data is only acceptable if the conditions specified in paragraph 7 are adhered to. These conditions are as follows:

(a) the data controller must accurately record information obtained;

(b) the data controller must take reasonable steps to ensure the accuracy of the data; and

(c) when informed that the data are inaccurate, the data controller must note this fact on the data.

The steps that the data controller must take in ensuring the accuracy of the data depend on the individual circumstances of the case. It is clear that the greater the chance of risking the rights and freedoms of the individual, the greater the steps must be in ensuring that the data are accurate.

Data controllers are required to keep data up-to-date "where necessary". In practice it is in a data controller's interest to ensure that data are kept up-to-date or its value will be partially lost. It is therefore important that regular reviews are carried out and recorded.

An enforcement notice under section 40(4) may be served in respect of a contravention of this principle.

Breach of this principle may entitle an individual to seek compensation for any damage, distress or loss suffered as a result of inaccurate data processed by a data controller (section 13).

The sixth principle

8. A person is to be regarded as contravening the sixth principle if, but only if—
(a) he contravenes section 7 by failing to supply information in accordance with that section,
(b) he contravenes section 10 by failing to comply with a notice given under subsection (1) of that section to the extent that the notice is justified or by failing to give a notice under subsection (3) of that section,
(c) he contravenes section 11 by failing to comply with a notice given under subsection (1) of that section,
(d) he contravenes section 12 by failing to comply with a notice given under subsection (1) or (2)(b) of that section or by failing to give a notification under subsection (2)(a) of that section or a notice under subsection (3) of that section, or
¹(e) he contravenes section 12A by failing to comply with a notice given under subsection (1) of that section to the extent that the notice is justified.

NOTE
¹Paragraph 8(e) and the word "or" immediately preceding it inserted by the Data Protection Act 1998 (c.29), Sched. 13, para. 5.

GENERAL NOTE
This principle empowers the Information Commissioner to enforce the rights of data subjects (under Part II of the Act) against data controllers. A contravention of section 7 (subject access), section 10 (the right to prevent processing which might cause damage and distress), section 11 (the right to prevent processing for the purposes of direct marketing) or section 12 (the rights regarding automated decision making) is held to be in contravention of the sixth data protection principle.

The seventh principle

9. Having regard to the state of technological development and the cost of implementing any measures, the measures must ensure a level of security appropriate to—
(a) the harm that might result from such unauthorised or unlawful processing or accidental loss, destruction or damage as are mentioned in the seventh principle, and
(b) the nature of the data to be protected.
10. The data controller must take reasonable steps to ensure the reliability of any employees of his who have access to the personal data.
11. Where processing of personal data is carried out by a data processor on behalf of a data controller, the data controller must in order to comply with the seventh principle—
(a) choose a data processor providing sufficient guarantees in respect of the technical and organisational security measures governing the processing to be carried out, and
(b) take reasonable steps to ensure compliance with those measures.
12. Where processing of personal data is carried out by a data processor on behalf of a data controller; the data controller is not to be regarded as complying with the seventh principle unless—
(a) the processing is carried out under a contract—
(i) which is made or evidenced in writing, and
(ii) under which the data processor is to act only on instructions from the data controller, and
(b) the contract requires the data processor to comply with obligations equivalent to those imposed on a data controller by the seventh principle.

GENERAL NOTE
Technical measures include passwords, virus scanning software, firewalls, etc. Organisational measures include the physical security of premises, training of staff, and the monitoring of data within the business of the data controller.
The more sensitive the data and the more harm that may result from an unauthorised disclosure, the more stringent the security measures should be. When considering security measures, a data controller must take into account the technological measures available and the cost of implementing them. A data controller is not expected to implement expensive state-of-the-art technological measures unless the level of sensitivity of the data demands it.
Data controllers must ensure that any member of staff allowed access to personal data is reliable and trustworthy. This means that data protection guidance in staff manuals and data protection training courses should be provided for employees. Any deliberate or negligent contravention of

the Act should be a specific staff disciplinary offence, resulting in a disciplinary hearing. Companies are advised to appoint a data protection officer who should:

(a) organise training for staff;

(b) draft a data protection policy;

(c) be the point of contact within the organisation for the Information Commissioner and for members of staff to approach with queries on data protection; and

(d) assist in the disciplinary process and assess the likely harm that any contravention of the Act by an employee may have caused.

Data controllers should also carry out a risk assessment exercise to check that precautions against theft, fire or natural disasters are adequate. Also, the storage and disposal of items holding personal data, such as computer disks or printouts, should be carefully considered.

Any processing carried out by data processors on behalf of a data controller is dealt with in paragraphs 11 and 12. The Information Commissioner has no power to enforce the provisions of the Act upon data processors if they are found to be processing unlawfully or unfairly. This is because under section 4(3) only data controllers have a duty to comply with the principles. However, it is open to the Information Commissioner to take enforcement action against a data controller if a data processor breaches the Act. The data controller would subsequently have a right of action against the data processor for breach of contract.

A data processor is broadly defined due to the wide definition of "processing" in section 1(1). A data processor is anyone who carries out any processing of personal data on behalf of a data controller. To ensure compliance with the principles, a data controller should obtain a guarantee from the data processor that it will employ adequate security and organisational measures with regard to the personal data. To ensure the data processor's compliance with the guarantee, the data controller should obtain a contractual right to audit the data processor's security and organisational measures.

The contract between a data controller and its data processor must be in writing and require the data processor to comply with the same obligations that are imposed on the data controller by the seventh principle. The written contract should also stipulate that the data processor is only to act on the instructions of the data controller.

The eighth principle

13. An adequate level of protection is one which is adequate in all the circumstances of the case, having regard in particular to—

(a) the nature of the personal data,

(b) the country or territory of origin of the information contained in the data,

(c) the country or territory of final destination of that information,

(d) the purposes for which and period during which the data are intended to be processed,

(e) the law in force in the country or territory in question,

(f) the international obligations of that country or territory,

(g) any relevant codes of conduct or other rules which are enforceable in that country or territory (whether generally or by arrangement in particular cases), and

(h) any security measures taken in respect of the data in that country or territory.

14. The eighth principle does not apply to a transfer falling within any paragraph of Schedule 4, except in such circumstances and to such extent as the Secretary of State may by order provide.

15.—(1) Where—

(a) in any proceedings under this Act any question arises as to whether the requirement of the eighth principle as to an adequate level of protection is met in relation to the transfer of any personal data to a country or territory outside the European Economic Area, and

(b) a Community finding has been made in relation to transfers of the kind in question,

that question is to be determined in accordance with that finding.

(2) In sub-paragraph (1) "Community finding" means a finding of the European Commission, under the procedure provided for in Article 31(2) of the Data Protection Directive, that a country or territory outside the European Economic Area does, or does not, ensure an adequate level of protection within the meaning of Article 25(2) of the Directive.

GENERAL NOTE

The eighth principle is in implementation of Article 25 of the Directive and prohibits the transfer of personal data to countries outwith the European Economic Area (EEA) unless that country has in place an adequate level of protection. To decide whether a country has an adequate level of protection a data controller must consider several factors. He must first find out if the European Commission has made a conclusive finding ("Community finding" – paragraph 15) as to the level of protection in a specific country. The finding will state whether or not the third country

Data Protection Act 1998

Data Protection Act 1998

has measures in place that are adequate within the meaning of Article 25(1) of the Directive. Paragraph 13 sets out the criteria for what is considered to denote an adequate level of protection.

If there is no Community finding it is up to the data controller to consider whether the country in question has adequate levels of protection and to carry out a risk assessment. The criteria in paragraph 13 are designed to offer guidance to the data controller in making this determination. The list is not designed to be exhaustive, and can be divided into two categories. The first is general criteria relating to the data and the circumstances surrounding the transfer. The second is the legal criteria relating to the law of the third country, its international obligations, etc.

The level of protection is not required to be equivalent to the protection offered in the United Kingdom, but it must be adequate.

SCHEDULE 2

Section 4(3)

CONDITIONS RELEVANT FOR PURPOSES OF THE FIRST PRINCIPLE: PROCESSING OF ANY PERSONAL DATA

1. The data subject has given his consent to the processing.
2. The processing is necessary—
(a) for the performance of a contract to which the data subject is a party, or
(b) for the taking of steps at the request of the data subject with a view to entering into a contract.
3. The processing is necessary for compliance with any legal obligation to which the data controller is subject, other than an obligation imposed by contract.
4. The processing is necessary in order to protect the vital interests of the data subject.
5. The processing is necessary—
(a) for the administration of justice,
(b) for the exercise of any functions conferred on any person by or under any enactment,
(c) for the exercise of any functions of the Crown, a Minister of the Crown or a government department, or
(d) for the exercise of any other functions of a public nature exercised in the public interest by any person.
6.—(1) The processing is necessary for the purposes of legitimate interests pursued by the data controller or by the third party or parties to whom the data are disclosed, except where the processing is unwarranted in any particular case by reason of prejudice to the rights and freedoms or legitimate interests of the data subject.
(2) The Secretary of State may by order specify particular circumstances in which this condition is, or is not, to be taken to be satisfied.

GENERAL NOTE

Schedules 2 and 3 form part of the first principle, which states that personal data must be processed fairly and lawfully. To achieve this a data controller must follow the fair processing code set out in paragraphs 1 to 4 of Schedule 1, and also must comply with at least one condition from Schedule 2 (with regard to personal data) or at least one condition from each of Schedules 2 and 3 (with regard to sensitive personal data).

Paragraph 1

Paragraph 1 contains the first condition. The data controller may process personal data as long as the data subject has consented to the processing. Although "consent" is not defined, it is generally accepted that the courts will determine what the term means in the particular circumstances of the case. The Directive gives some guidance as it defined "consent" as "any freely given specific and informed indication of [the data subject's] wishes by which he signifies his agreement to personal data relating to him being processed" (Article 2(h)). The Act must therefore be interpreted in accordance with the Directive when considering the issue of consent. The Information Commissioner's Guidelines also offer some interpretation as it is stated "data controllers cannot infer consent from non-response to a communication, for example from a customer's failure to return or to respond to a leaflet".

It is clear that consent requires some positive indication by the data subject. Consent can be revoked once given, although if the data subject gives his consent as part of a contract, its revocation would be a contractual issue for the parties to agree upon.

80

Schedules

Paragraph 2

Paragraph 2 relates to two separate but related situations. The first situation is when the processing is considered necessary for the performance of a contract to which the data subject is a party. An example is an employment contract. A personnel department processing monthly salary details should not have to obtain subject consent every month. Another example is where the customer's details require to be processed for the delivery of goods or services. It is important that the processing is "necessary" for the performance of the contract, and that data controllers do not carry out any other unnecessary processing.

The second situation addressed in paragraph 2 is where the processing is necessary to take steps at the request of the data subject to enter into a contract. An example is when a data subject applies for credit and his personal data would then be required to be processed for a credit check with a credit reference company. Without this form of processing no credit agreements could be entered into and therefore the processing is considered necessary. The data controller must not carry out any additional processing other than that which satisfies the purpose of the processing.

Paragraph 3

Paragraph 3 allows processing to be carried out where it is necessary to comply with any legal obligations of the data controller other than processing required under a contract. For example, an employer must process personal data in relation to PAYE and National Insurance obligations. Data controllers may also be required to process personal data to comply with the Money Laundering Regulations. The reason for the use of the words "other than an obligation imposed by contract" is to prevent the situation where a data controller enters into a contract with another person allowing him to process a third party's personal data without that third party's knowledge or consent.

Paragraph 4

Paragraph 4 allows processing to be carried out when it is considered necessary to protect the vital interests of a data subject. The Act does not define "vital interests" although the Information Commissioner has advised that reliance on this particular condition "may only be claimed where the processing is necessary for matters of life and death, for example, the disclosure of a data subject's medical history to a hospital casualty department treating the data subject after a serious road accident" (Guidelines, Chapter 3, paragraph 1.2). Practically, this condition is likely to have limited application as it is more likely to refer to the processing of sensitive personal data and a further condition under Schedule 3 will also require to be satisfied.

Paragraph 5

Paragraph 5, subparagraphs (a) to (c) allow processing of personal data by the courts, any person exercising statutory functions and the government. Subparagraph (d) is broader and allows processing of personal data by any person exercising public functions in the interests of the public. Again this condition will only justify processing which is necessary and anything beyond what is necessary must be satisfied using one of the other conditions.

Paragraph 6

Paragraph 6(1) allows processing to be carried out when it is considered to be in the legitimate interests of the data controller or a third party to whom the data are disclosed except where the rights and freedoms or legitimate interests of the data subject are likely to be infringed. "Legitimate interests" is not defined and it is likely that the extent of what is considered to be a legitimate interest will be decided on a case-by-case basis. An individual's rights and freedoms are likely to include those contained in the European Convention for the Protection of Human Rights and Fundamental Freedoms (Cmd. 8969) and the Human Rights Act 1998.

Data controllers should satisfy themselves when disclosing personal data to third parties that any consequential processing will not have an adverse effect on the legitimate interests of the data subject.

Further guidance may be given here if the Secretary of State makes an order specifying when this condition is satisfied.

SCHEDULE 3

Section 4(3)

CONDITIONS RELEVANT FOR PURPOSES OF THE FIRST PRINCIPLE: PROCESSING OF SENSITIVE PERSONAL DATA

1. The data subject has given his explicit consent to the processing of the personal data.

2.—(1) The processing is necessary for the purposes of exercising or performing any right or obligation which is conferred or imposed by law on the data controller in connection with employment.

(2) The Secretary of State may by order—

(a) exclude the application of sub-paragraph (1) in such cases as may be specified, or

(b) provide that, in such cases as may be specified, the condition in sub-paragraph (1) is not to be regarded as satisfied unless such further conditions as may be specified in the order are also satisfied.

3. The processing is necessary—

(a) in order to protect the vital interests of the data subject or another person, in a case where—

    (i) consent cannot be given by or on behalf of the data subject, or

    (ii) the data controller cannot reasonably be expected to obtain the consent of the data subject, or

(b) in order to protect the vital interests of another person, in a case where consent by or on behalf of the data subject has been unreasonably withheld.

4. The processing—

(a) is carried out in the course of its legitimate activities by any body or association which—

    (i) is not established or conducted for profit, and

    (ii) exists for political, philosophical, religious or trade-union purposes,

(b) is carried out with appropriate safeguards for the rights and freedoms of data subjects,

(c) relates only to individuals who either are members of the body or association or have regular contact with it in connection with its purposes, and

(d) does not involve disclosure of the personal data to a third party without the consent of the data subject

5. The information contained in the personal data has been made public as a result of steps deliberately taken by the data subject.

6. The processing—

(a) is necessary for the purpose of, or in connection with, any legal proceedings (including prospective legal proceedings),

(b) is necessary for the purpose of obtaining legal advice, or

(c) is otherwise necessary for the purposes of establishing, exercising or defending legal rights.

7.—(1) The processing is necessary—

(a) for the administration of justice,

(b) for the exercise of any functions conferred on any person by or under an enactment, or

(c) for the exercise of any functions of the Crown, a Minister of the Crown or a government department.

(2) The Secretary of State may by order—

(a) exclude the application of sub-paragraph (1) in such cases as may be specified, or

(b) provide that, in such cases as may be specified, the condition in sub-paragraph (1) is not to be regarded as satisfied unless such further conditions as may be specified in the order are also satisfied.

8.—(1) The processing is necessary for medical purposes and is undertaken by—

(a) a health professional, or

(b) a person who in the circumstances owes a duty of confidentiality which is equivalent to that which would arise if that person were a health professional.

(2) In this paragraph "medical purposes" includes the purposes of preventative medicine, medical diagnosis, medical research, the provision of care and treatment and the management of health care services.

9.—(1) The processing—

(a) is of sensitive personal data consisting of information as to racial or ethnic origin,

(b) is necessary for the purpose of identifying or keeping under review the existence or absence of equality of opportunity or treatment between persons of different racial or ethnic origins, with a view to enabling such equality to be promoted or maintained, and

(c) is carried out with appropriate safeguards for the rights and freedoms of data subjects.

(2) The Secretary of State may by order specify circumstances in which processing falling within sub-paragraph (1)(a) and (b) is, or is not, to be taken for the purposes of sub-paragraph (1)(c) to be carried out with appropriate safeguards for the rights and freedoms of data subjects.

10. The personal data are processed in circumstances specified in an order made by the Secretary of State for the purposes of this paragraph.

GENERAL NOTE

Additional safeguards are necessary in relation to sensitive personal data because such data "are capable by their nature of infringing fundamental freedoms or privacy" (Directive, Article 33).

These safeguards are contained in the first principle that requires sensitive personal data to be processed in compliance with one of the conditions in Schedules 2 and 3. If a data controller cannot comply with any of these conditions he is unable to process the data.

Paragraph 1

Paragraph 1 is similar to paragraph 1 of Schedule 2, with the addition of the word "explicit". The Information Commissioner's Guidelines state, "the use of the word 'explicit' suggests that the consent of the data subject should be absolutely clear" (Chapter 3, paragraph 1.6). The Information Commissioner has indicated that "explicit consent" need not be in writing provided that it is unequivocal, and data controllers are advised to "consider the extent to which the use of personal data by them is or is not reasonably foreseeable by data subjects" (Guidelines, Chapter 3, paragraph 1.6).

The information which must be given to the data subject to obtain his explicit consent should state that sensitive personal data will be processed, and a description of the sensitive personal data should also be given. In addition, the purpose of the processing together with information as to whether or not the data are to be disclosed to third parties must also be provided to the data subject.

Explicit consent should be informed consent and should be reasonably current. The consent should also be freely given or will not be effective. For example, if a person applying for a job is asked for his consent to process his personal data as a condition of his employment, that consent is not considered to be freely given and the data controller should not process that data.

Paragraph 2

Paragraph 2 enables a data controller to process sensitive personal data where it is necessary to exercise or perform any right or obligation conferred or imposed by law on him, in relation to employment matters. This condition allows personnel departments to carry on most forms of processing, as long as it is necessary and required by law. It will not include processing which the employer simply wishes to carry out for his own purposes.

The Secretary of State has the power to prevent processing of sensitive personal data in some circumstances, or to impose additional conditions. This is to ensure that where the law does not provide sufficient safeguards in a particular area, these can be introduced to further protect the rights and freedoms of the individual.

Paragraph 3

Paragraph 3 allows processing of certain sensitive personal data where it is carried out to protect the "vital interests" of any individual and when subject consent cannot be obtained or is being unreasonably withheld. The processing must always be "necessary". In practice it is likely that this condition will have limited application, except perhaps in situations involving the processing of medical information or in emergency situations.

Paragraph 4

Paragraph 4 allows processing of sensitive personal data to be carried out by certain non-profit making organisations. However, there are five requirements set out, all of which must be adhered to, before this condition can apply:

(a) the processing must be carried out in the course of the organisation's "legitimate activities";

(b) the organisation must not be profit making;

(c) the processing must be carried out with appropriate safeguards for the rights and freedoms of data subjects;

(d) the processing must only relate to members or individuals who have regular contact with the organisation; and

(e) the processing must not involve disclosure of personal data to a third party without the consent of the data subject.

It is logical that certain organisations, such as trade unions, political and religious organisations, need to be provided with special rights for the processing of sensitive personal data because the very fact that their members share their beliefs falls within the definition of "sensitive personal data". These groups should however be careful not to process any personal data of those who are not members such as members' spouses or children. Any groups that are established in order to make a profit are excluded from benefiting from this condition.

Paragraph 5

Paragraph 5 relates to the situation where the data subject has publicised information about himself that would be regarded as sensitive personal data, which is subsequently to be processed by the data controller. This would apply, for example, where a politician has made public his political beliefs. However, the condition does not apply when the information is made public by someone other than the data subject and without the data subject's consent, such as publication by a newspaper.

Paragraph 6

Paragraph 6 allows sensitive personal data to be processed where it is necessary for any legal proceedings, for the purpose of obtaining of legal advice or in order to exercise, establish or defend legal rights. The application of this condition extends not only to data subjects but also in relation to other individuals.

Paragraph 7

Paragraph 7 is similar to the condition in Schedule 2, paragraph 5, although it is more restrictive. It allows the processing of sensitive personal data where it is necessary for the administration of justice, for the exercise of any statutory functions, or by the government. However, it cannot be justified as being in the interests of the public. Under paragraph 7(2) the Secretary of State can make an order prohibiting certain processing where the public sector processing may not involve sensitive personal data. Alternatively the Secretary of State can impose further conditions to provide additional safeguards.

Paragraph 8

Paragraph 8 allows processing of sensitive personal data where this is considered necessary for "medical purposes" (defined in subparagraph (2)). This condition is subject to the safeguard in paragraph 8(1) that permits the processing to be carried out only by a "health professional" or a person who, depending on the circumstances of the processing, is deemed to owe an equivalent duty of confidentiality to that of a health professional. "Health professional" is defined in section 69(1).

Paragraph 9

Paragraph 9 allows processing of sensitive personal data relating to racial or ethnic origin to be carried out if all three conditions set out in paragraph 9(1) are met. The "appropriate safeguards" for the rights and freedoms of the data subject are to be determined by the Secretary of State by order. The Secretary of State may also by order keep under review and exercise control over the processing of data for these purposes to allow appropriate safeguards to remain in place and be put in place in line with developments in the law relating to the promotion of racial and ethnic equality.

Paragraph 10

Paragraph 10 grants the Secretary of State the power to make further orders in relation to the conditions for the processing of sensitive personal data. It was proposed that financial institutions be allowed to continue processing information about criminal records to prevent or detect fraud. It is also anticipated that political parties will be allowed to process information about the political opinions in relation to canvassing. See the Data Protection (Processing of Sensitive Personal Data) Order 2000 (S.I. 2000 No. 417).

SCHEDULE 4

Section 4(3)

CASES WHERE THE EIGHTH PRINCIPLE DOES NOT APPLY

1. The data subject has given his consent to the transfer.
2. The transfer is necessary—
(a) for the performance of a contract between the data subject and the data controller, or
(b) for the taking of steps at the request of the data subject with a view to his entering into a contract with the data controller.
3. The transfer is necessary—
(a) for the conclusion of a contract between the data controller and a person other than the data subject which—
    (i) is entered into at the request of the data subject, or
    (ii) is in the interests of the data subject, or
(b) for the performance of such a contract.
4.—(1) The transfer is necessary for reasons of substantial public interest.
(2) The Secretary of State may by order specify—

(a) circumstances in which a transfer is to be taken for the purposes of sub-paragraph (1) to be necessary for reasons of substantial public interest, and

(b) circumstances in which a transfer which is not required by or under an enactment is not to be taken for the purpose of sub-paragraph (1) to be necessary for reasons of substantial public interest.

5. The transfer—

(a) is necessary for the purpose of, or in connection with, any legal proceedings (including prospective legal proceedings),

(b) is necessary for the purpose of obtaining legal advice, or

(c) is otherwise necessary for the purposes of establishing, exercising or defending legal rights.

6. The transfer is necessary in order to protect the vital interests of the data subject.

7. The transfer is of part of the personal data on a public register and any conditions subject to which the register is open to inspection are complied with by any person to whom the data are or may be disclosed after the transfer.

8. The transfer is made on terms which are of a kind approved by the Commissioner as ensuring adequate safeguards for the rights and freedoms of data subjects.

9. The transfer has been authorised by the Commissioner as being made in such a manner as to ensure adequate safeguards for the rights and freedoms of data subjects

GENERAL NOTE
The eighth data protection principle introduces a prohibition against the transfer of personal data outwith the EEA unless the specific country in question affords an adequate level of protection for the rights and freedoms of individuals with regard to the processing. In Schedule 1, Part II, paragraph 14, the eighth principle is said not to apply to any transfers falling under any provision of Schedule 4. Therefore a data controller does not have to concern itself with cross-border transfers of data where the processing complies with one of the conditions of Schedule 4.

Paragraph 1
Paragraph 1 provides that the eighth principle will not apply if the data subject has consented to the transfer of personal data to a third country. There is no mention of "explicit consent" so it can be inferred that implied consent is sufficient. However, the Information Commissioner's Guidelines suggest that obtaining blanket consent from data subjects is unlikely to be sufficient (Guidelines, Chapter 3, paragraph 1.6, via paragraph 8.4). It is therefore wise for data controllers who transfer data to obtain consent from the relevant data subjects to transfer their personal data to particular countries that are specified. Such consent could be obtained via the subject information notice.

Paragraph 2
Paragraph 2 provides that the eighth principle will not apply if the transfer is necessary for the performance of a contract between the data subject and the data controller or for the taking of steps at the request of the data subject in contemplation of entering a contract with the data subject. The first situation may apply where the data controller is arranging travel for the data subject and needs to transfer data to a hotel situated in a country outwith the EEA. In both situations the transfer of data must be "necessary".

Paragraph 3
Paragraph 3 provides that the eighth principle will not apply where the transfer of data is necessary for the conclusion of a contract between the data controller and an individual other than the data subject which is either entered into at the data subject's request or is in the interests of the data subject, or for the performance of such a contract. This provision was inserted specifically for credit card transactions where the contract is between a foreign merchant and the credit card company and is specifically at the request of the data subject. The request is made when the data subject hands over his card in payment.

Paragraph 4
Paragraph 4 provides that the eighth principle will not apply in situations where the transfer is necessary for reasons of "substantial public interest". It is likely that the courts will interpret the meaning of "substantial public interest" taking into account the particular circumstances of the case.

Paragraph 5
Paragraph 5 provides that the eighth principle will not apply in situations where the transfer is necessary for any legal proceedings, for the obtaining of legal advice or in order to exercise, establish or defend legal rights.

Paragraph 6

Paragraph 6 provides that the eighth principle will not apply in situations where the processing is necessary to protect the vital interests of the data subject.

Paragraph 7

Paragraph 7 provides that the eighth principle will not apply where the transfer is of personal data extracted from a register intended to provide information to the public and which is openly accessible to the public. This is subject to the condition that the recipient of the personal data must comply with any conditions attaching to the register. The most obvious application of this provision is in relation to the electoral register or the companies register.

Paragraph 8

Paragraph 8 provides that the eighth principle will not apply in situations where the transfer is in terms approved by the Information Commissioner. The only basis upon which the Information Commissioner is likely to approve terms (*e.g.* model contract clauses) is where data controllers ensure that adequate safeguards are in place for the rights and freedoms of data subjects. The Information Commissioner is only likely to issue a small number of model clauses to cover widely used processing activities.

Paragraph 9

Paragraph 9 provides that the eighth principle will not apply in situations where the transfer has been authorised by the Information Commissioner as having adequate safeguards for the rights and freedoms of data subjects. It is likely that the power conferred on the Information Commissioner to authorise transfers will not be used often as the Information Commissioner has already expressed that this should be used as a last resort, once all other derogations have been considered.

SCHEDULE 5

Section 4(3)

THE DATA PROTECTION COMMISSIONER AND THE DATA PROTECTION TRIBUNAL

PART I

THE COMMISSIONER

Status and capacity

1.—(1) The corporation sole by the name of the Data Protection Registrar established by the Data Protection Act 1984 shall continue in existence by the name of [the Information Commissioner]'.

(2) The Commissioner and his officers and staff are not to be regarded as servants or agents of the Crown.

Tenure of office

2.—(1) Subject to the provisions of this paragraph, the Commissioner shall hold office for such term not exceeding five years as may be determined at the time of his appointment.

(2) The Commissioner may be relieved of his office by Her Majesty at his own request.

(3) The Commissioner may be removed from office by Her Majesty in pursuance of an Address from both Houses of Parliament.

(4) The Commissioner shall in any case vacate his office—

(a) on completing the year of service in which he attains the age of sixty- five years, or

(b) if earlier, on completing his fifteenth year of service.

(5) Subject to sub-paragraph (4), a person who ceases to be Commissioner on the expiration of his term of office shall be eligible for re-appointment, but a person may not be re-appointed for a third or subsequent term as Commissioner unless, by reason of special circumstances, the person's re-appointment for such a term is desirable in the public interest.

Schedules

Salary etc.

3.—(1) There shall be paid—

(a) to the Commissioner such salary, and

(b) to or in respect of the Commissioner such pension,

as may be specified by a resolution of the House of Commons.

(2) A resolution for the purposes of this paragraph may—

(a) specify the salary or pension,

(b) provide that the salary or pension is to be the same as, or calculated on the same basis as, that payable to, or to or in respect of, a person employed in a specified office under, or in a specified capacity in the service of, the Crown, or

(c) specify the salary or pension and provide for it to be increased by reference to such variables as may be specified in the resolution.

(3) A resolution for the purposes of this paragraph may take effect from the date on which it is passed or from any earlier or later date specified in the resolution.

(4) A resolution for the purposes of this paragraph may make different provision in relation to the pension payable to or in respect of different holders of the office of Commissioner.

(5) Any salary or pension payable under this paragraph shall be charged on and issued out of the Consolidated Fund.

(6) In this paragraph "pension" includes an allowance or gratuity and any reference to the payment of a pension includes a reference to the making of payments towards the provision of a pension.

Officers and staff

4.—(1) The Commissioner—

(a) shall appoint a deputy commissioner or two deputy commissioners, and

(b) may appoint such number of other officers and staff as he may determine.

²(1A) The Commissioner shall, when appointing any second deputy commissioner, specify which of the Commissioner's functions are to be performed, in the circumstances referred to in paragraph 5(1), by each of the deputy commissioners.

(2) The remuneration and other conditions of service of the persons appointed under this paragraph shall be determined by the Commissioner.

(3) The Commissioner may pay such pensions, allowances or gratuities to or in respect of the persons appointed under this paragraph, or make such payments towards the provision of such pensions, allowances or gratuities, as he may determine.

(4) The references in sub-paragraph (3) to pensions, allowances or gratuities to or in respect of the persons appointed under this paragraph include references to pensions, allowances or gratuities by way of compensation to or in respect of any of those persons who suffer loss of office or employment.

(5) Any determination under sub-paragraph (1)(b), (2) or (3) shall require the approval of the Secretary of State.

(6) The Employers' Liability (Compulsory Insurance) Act 1969 shall not require insurance to be effected by the Commissioner.

5.—(1) The deputy commissioner or deputy commissioners shall perform the functions conferred by this Act or the Freedom of Information Act 2000 on the Commissioner during any vacancy in that office or at any time when the Commissioner is for any reason unable to act.

(2) Without prejudice to sub-paragraph (1), any functions of the Commissioner under this Act [or the Freedom of Information Act 2000]³ may, to the extent authorised by him, be performed by any of his officers or staff.

Authentication of seal of the Commissioner

6. The application of the seal of the Commissioner shall be authenticated by his signature or by the signature of some other person authorised for the purpose.

Presumption of authenticity of documents issued by the Commissioner

7. Any document purporting to be an instrument issued by the Commissioner and to be duly executed under the Commissioner's seal or to be signed by or on behalf of the Commissioner shall be received in evidence and shall be deemed to be such an instrument unless the contrary is shown.

Money

8. The Secretary of State may make payments to the Commissioner out of money provided by Parliament.

9.—(1) All fees and other sums received by the Commissioner in the exercise of his functions under this Act[, under section 159 of the Consumer Credit Act 1974 or under the Freedom of Information Act 2000][1] shall be paid by him to the Secretary of State.

(2) Sub-paragraph (1) shall not apply where the Secretary of State, with the consent of the Treasury, otherwise directs.

(3) Any sums received by the Secretary of State under sub-paragraph (1) shall be paid into the Consolidated Fund.

Accounts

10.—(1) It shall be the duty of the Commissioner—

(a) to keep proper accounts and other records in relation to the accounts,

(b) to prepare in respect of each financial year a statement of account in such form as the Secretary of State may direct, and

(c) to send copies of that statement to the Comptroller and Auditor General on or before 31st August next following the end of the year to which the statement relates or on or before such earlier date after the end of that year as the Treasury may direct.

(2) The Comptroller and Auditor General shall examine and certify any statement sent to him under this paragraph and lay copies of it together with his report thereon before each House of Parliament.

(3) In this paragraph "financial year" means a period of twelve months beginning with 1st April.

Application of Part I in Scotland

11. Paragraphs 1(1), 6 and 7 do not extend to Scotland.

NOTES
[1]Words substituted by the Freedom of Information Act 2000 (c.36), Sched. 2, para. 15(2).
[2]Added by the Freedom of Information Act 2000 (c.36), Sched. 2, para. 20(3).
[3]Words added by the Freedom of Information Act 2000 (c.36), Sched. 2, para. 21(3).
[4]Words substituted by the Freedom of Information Act 2000 (c.36), Sched. 2, para. 22.

GENERAL NOTE
The appointment of the Commissioner who since January 30, 2001 is now called the Information Commissioner (amended by the Freedom of Information Act 2000), was a result of Article 28(1) of the Directive which required Member States to appoint a supervisory body acting with "complete independence in exercising the functions entrusted to [it]". The Information Commissioner is the supervisory body for the United Kingdom, taking over from the Data Protection Registrar under the 1984 Act. The Information Commissioner is completely independent and is not an agent of the Crown. The Information Commissioner may only be removed from office by the Queen acting in pursuance of an address by both Houses of Parliament (paragraph 2(3)).

Paragraph 4
Paragraph 4 enables the Information Commissioner to appoint one or two deputy Commissioners, other officers and staff. The Information Commissioner determines salaries of staff. The Information Commissioner's office receives funding from Parliament in addition to the income received from the system of registration (notification). The Freedom of Information Act 2000 inserted a new paragraph 4(1A) enabling the Information Commissioner to specify the functions to be performed by the deputy Commissioners.

Paragraph 11
Paragraph 11 states that certain paragraphs in this part of Schedule 5 (namely paragraphs 1(1), 6 and 7) do not apply to Scotland. This is due to the fact that the Requirements of Writing (Scotland) Act 1995 governs the authentication of documents in Scotland.

Schedules

THE TRIBUNAL

Tenure of office

12.—(1) Subject to the following provisions of this paragraph, a member of the Tribunal shall hold and vacate his office in accordance with the terms of his appointment and shall, on ceasing to hold office, be eligible for re-appointment.

(2) Any member of the Tribunal may at any time resign his office by notice in writing to the Lord Chancellor (in the case of the chairman or a deputy chairman) or to the Secretary of State (in the case of any other member).

(3) A person who is the chairman or deputy chairman of the Tribunal shall vacate his office on the day on which he attains the age of seventy years; but this sub-paragraph is subject to section 26(4) to (6) of the Judicial Pensions and Retirement Act 1993 (power to authorise continuance in office up to the age of seventy-five years).

Salary etc.

13. The Secretary of State shall pay to the members of the Tribunal out of money provided by Parliament such remuneration and allowances as he may determine.

Officers and staff

14. The Secretary of State may provide the Tribunal with such officers and staff as he thinks necessary for the proper discharge of its functions.

Expenses

15. Such expenses of the Tribunal as the Secretary of State may determine shall be defrayed by the Secretary of State out of money provided by Parliament.

GENERAL NOTE

The constitution of the Tribunal is determined by section 6(4). The Tribunal must include a panel of lay members who should be competent, informed and representative of the businesses and organisations that are affected by the data protection regime. Legally qualified members of the Tribunal must have been so qualified for at least seven years (section 6(5)). The Tribunal will consist of a chairperson, deputy chairperson and other members (section 6(4)).

Part II of Schedule 5 sets out the administrative details of the Tribunal, including salaries and tenure of office. There are no time limits in respect of periods of office, and these are subject only to the provisions on retirement contained in paragraph 3. The Secretary of State determines remuneration for the office holders within the Tribunal.

PART III

TRANSITIONAL PROVISIONS

16. *Repealed by the Freedom of Information Act 2000 (c.36), Sched. 8, para. 1.*
17. *Repealed by the Freedom of Information Act 2000 (c.36), Sched. 8, para. 1.*

SCHEDULE 6

Sections 28(12), 48(5)

APPEAL PROCEEDINGS

Hearing of appeals

1. For the purpose of hearing and determining appeals or any matter preliminary or incidental to an appeal the Tribunal shall sit at such times and in such places as the chairman or a deputy chairman may direct and may sit in two or more divisions.

Constitution of Tribunal in national security cases

2.—(1) The Lord Chancellor shall from time to time designate, from among the chairman and deputy chairman appointed by him under section 6(4)(a) and (b), those persons who are to be capable of hearing appeals under section 28(4) or (6) [or under section 60(1) or (4) of the Freedom of Information Act 2000]¹.

(2) A designation under sub-paragraph (1) may at any time be revoked by the Lord Chancellor.

3. In any case where the application of paragraph 6(1) is excluded by rules under paragraph 7, the Tribunal shall be duly constituted for an appeal under section 28(4) or (6) if it consists of three of the persons designated under paragraph 2(1), of whom one shall be designated by the Lord Chancellor to preside.

Constitution of Tribunal in other cases

4.—(1) Subject to any rules made under paragraph 7, the Tribunal shall be duly constituted for an appeal under section 48(1), (2) or (4) if it consists of—
  (a) the chairman or a deputy chairman (who shall preside), and
  (b) an equal number of the members appointed respectively in accordance with paragraphs (a) and (b) of section 6(6).

(2) The members who are to constitute the Tribunal in accordance with sub-paragraph (1) shall be nominated by the chairman or, if he is for any reason unable to act, by a deputy chairman.

Determination of questions by full Tribunal

5. The determination of any question before the Tribunal when constituted in accordance with paragraph 3 or 4 shall be according to the opinion of the majority of the members hearing the appeal.

Ex parte proceedings

6.—(1) Subject to any rules made under paragraph 7, the jurisdiction of the Tribunal in respect of an appeal under section 28(4) or (6) shall be exercised *ex parte* by one or more persons designated under paragraph 2(1).

(2) Subject to any rules made under paragraph 7, the jurisdiction of the Tribunal in respect of an appeal under section 48(3) shall be exercised *ex parte* by the chairman or a deputy chairman sitting alone.

Rules of procedure

7.—(1) The Secretary of State may make rules for [regulating—
  (a) the exercise of the rights of appeal conferred—
    (i) by sections 28(4) and (6) and 48, and
    (ii) by sections 57(1) and (2) and section 60(1) and (4) of the Freedom of Information Act 2000, and
  (b) the practice and procedure of the Tribunal.]²

(2) Rules under this paragraph may in particular make provision—
  (a) with respect to the period within which an appeal can be brought and the burden of proof on an appeal,
  ³(aa) for the joinder of any other person as a party to any proceedings on an appeal under the Freedom of Information Act 2000,
  ³(ab) for the hearing of an appeal under this Act with an appeal under the Freedom of Information Act 2000,
  (b) for the summoning (or, in Scotland, citation) of witnesses and the administration of oaths,
  (c) for securing the production of documents and material used for the processing of personal data,
  (d) for the inspection, examination, operation and testing of any equipment or material used in connection with the processing of personal data,
  (e) for the hearing of an appeal wholly or partly *in camera*,
  (f) for hearing an appeal in the absence of the appellant or for determining an appeal without a hearing,

(g) for enabling an appeal under section 48(1) against an information notice to be determined by the chairman or a deputy chairman,

(h) for enabling any matter preliminary or incidental to an appeal to be dealt with by the chairman or a deputy chairman,

(i) for the awarding of costs or, in Scotland, expenses,

(j) for the publication of reports of the Tribunal's decisions, and

(k) for conferring on the Tribunal such ancillary powers as the Secretary of State thinks necessary for the proper discharge of its functions.

(3) In making rules under this paragraph which relate to appeals under section 28(4) or (6) the Secretary of State shall have regard, in particular, to the need to secure that information is not disclosed contrary to the public interest.

Obstruction etc.

8.—(1) If any person is guilty of any act or omission in relation to proceedings before the Tribunal which, if those proceedings were proceedings before a court having power to commit for contempt, would constitute contempt of court, the Tribunal may certify the offence to the High Court or, in Scotland, the Court of Session.

(2) Where an offence is so certified, the court may inquire into the matter and, after hearing any witness who may be produced against or on behalf of the person charged with the offence, and after hearing any statement that may be offered in defence, deal with him in any manner in which it could deal with him if he had committed the like offence in relation to the court.

NOTES

[1]Words inserted by the Freedom of Information Act 2000 (c.36), Sched. 4, para. 1, effective May 14, 2001.

[2]Words substituted by the Freedom of Information Act 2000 (c.36), Sched. 4, para. 4(2), effective May 14, 2001.

[3]Added by the Freedom of Information Act 2000 (c.36), Sched. 4, para. 4(3), effective May 14, 2001.

GENERAL NOTE

Sections 48 and 28(12) should also be consulted in relation to this Schedule. Section 48 provides a right to appeal in respect of enforcement notices, information notices or special information notices, including the Information Commissioner's powers to vary or cancel an enforcement notice.

This Schedule deals with the procedural aspects of appeals to the Tribunal.

An alternative composition of the Tribunal is provided for in matters of national security and does not include lay members (paragraph 2).

The constitution of the Tribunal for other cases is set out in paragraph 4.

The Tribunal decides its judgments on a majority vote (subject to certain provisions relating to cases of national security).

Paragraph 6 also relates to *ex parte* proceedings. *Ex parte* proceedings mean proceedings brought by one party without the other party being involved.

Paragraph 8 provides an offence in relation to the Tribunal whereby any person who is guilty of an act or omission that would constitute contempt of court before a court, will be certified by the Tribunal to have committed a contempt of court as if the proceedings were in the High Court (England) or the Court of Session (Scotland).

SCHEDULE 7

Section 37

MISCELLANEOUS EXEMPTIONS

Confidential references given by the data controller

1. Personal data are exempt from section 7 if they consist of a reference given or to be given in confidence by the data controller for the purposes of—

(a) the education, training or employment, or prospective education, training or employment, of the data subject,

(b) the appointment, or prospective appointment, of the data subject to any office, or

(c) the provision, or prospective provision, by the data subject of any service.

Armed forces

2. Personal data are exempt from the subject information provisions in any case to the extent to which the application of those provisions would be likely to prejudice the combat effectiveness of any of the armed forces of the Crown.

Judicial appointments and honours

3. Personal data processed for the purposes of—

(a) assessing any person's suitability for judicial office or the office of Queen's Counsel, or

(b) the conferring by the Crown of any honour [or dignity]',

are exempt from the subject information provisions.

Crown employment and Crown or Ministerial appointments

²4.—(1) The Secretary of State may by order exempt from the subject information provisions personal data processed for the purposes of assessing any person's suitability for—

(a) employment by or under the Crown, or

(b) any office to which appointments are made by Her Majesty, by a Minister of the Crown or by a Northern Ireland authority.

(2) In this paragraph "Northern Ireland authority" means the First Minister, the deputy First Minister, a Northern Ireland Minister or a Northern Ireland department.

Management forecasts etc.

5. Personal data processed for the purposes of management forecasting or management planning to assist the data controller in the conduct of any business or other activity are exempt from the subject information provisions in any case to the extent to which the application of those provisions would be likely to prejudice the conduct of that business or other activity.

Corporate finance

6.—(1) Where personal data are processed for the purposes of, or in connection with, a corporate finance service provided by a relevant person—

(a) the data are exempt from the subject information provisions in any case to the extent to which either—

    (i) the application of those provisions to the data could affect the price of any instrument which is already in existence or is to be or may be created, or

    (ii) the data controller reasonably believes that the application of those provisions to the data could affect the price of any such instrument, and

(b) to the extent that the data are not exempt from the subject information provisions by virtue of paragraph (a), they are exempt from those provisions if the exemption is required for the purpose of safeguarding an important economic or financial interest of the United Kingdom.

(2) For the purposes of sub-paragraph (1)(b) the Secretary of State may by order specify—

(a) matters to be taken into account in determining whether exemption from the subject information provisions is required for the purpose of safeguarding an important economic or financial interest of the United Kingdom, or

(b) circumstances in which exemption from those provisions is, or is not, to be taken to be required for that purpose.

(3) In this paragraph—

"corporate finance service" means a service consisting in—

    (a) underwriting in respect of issues of, or the placing of issues of, any instrument,

    (b) advice to undertakings on capital structure, industrial strategy and related matters and advice and service relating to mergers and the purchase of undertakings, or

    (c) services relating to such underwriting as is mentioned in paragraph (a);

"instrument" means any instrument listed in section B of the Annex to the Council Directive on investment services in the securities field (93/22/EEC), as set out in Schedule 1 to the Investment Services Regulations 1995;

"price" includes value;

"relevant person" means—

  (a) any person who is authorised under Chapter III of Part I of the Financial Services Act 1986 or is an exempted person under Chapter IV of Part I of that Act,

  (b) any person who, but for Part III or IV of Schedule 1 to that Act, would require authorisation under that Act,

  (c) any European investment firm within the meaning given by Regulation 3 of the Investment Services Regulations 1995,

  (d) any person who, in the course of his employment, provides to his employer a service falling within paragraph (b) or (c) of the definition of "corporate finance service", or

  (e) any partner who provides to other partners in the partnership a service falling within either of those paragraphs.

Negotiations

7. Personal data which consist of records of the intentions of the data controller in relation to any negotiations with the data subject are exempt from the subject information provisions in any case to the extent to which the application of those provisions would be likely to prejudice those negotiations.

Examination marks

8.—(1) Section 7 shall have effect subject to the provisions of sub-paragraphs (2) to (4) in the case of personal data consisting of marks or other information processed by a data controller—

  (a) for the purpose of determining the results of an academic, professional or other examination or of enabling the results of any such examination to be determined, or

  (b) in consequence of the determination of any such results.

(2) Where the relevant day falls before the day on which the results of the examination are announced, the period mentioned in section 7(8) shall be extended until—

  (a) the end of five months beginning with the relevant day, or

  (b) the end of forty days beginning with the date of the announcement,

whichever is the earlier.

(3) Where by virtue of sub-paragraph (2) a period longer than the prescribed period elapses after the relevant day before the request is complied with, the information to be supplied pursuant to the request shall be supplied both by reference to the data in question at the time when the request is received and (if different) by reference to the data as from time to time held in the period beginning when the request is received and ending when it is complied with.

(4) For the purposes of this paragraph the results of an examination shall be treated as announced when they are first published or (if not published) when they are first made available or communicated to the candidate in question.

(5) In this paragraph—

"examination" includes any process for determining the knowledge, intelligence, skill or ability of a candidate by reference to his performance in any test, work or other activity;

"the prescribed period" means forty days or such other period as is for the time being prescribed under section 7 in relation to the personal data in question;

"relevant day" has the same meaning as in section 7.

Examination scripts etc.

9.—(1) Personal data consisting of information recorded by candidates during an academic, professional or other examination are exempt from section 7.

(2) In this paragraph "examination" has the same meaning as in paragraph 8.

Legal professional privilege

10. Personal data are exempt from the subject information provisions if the data consist of information in respect of which a claim to legal professional privilege [or, in Scotland, to confidentiality of communications]¹ could be maintained in legal proceedings.

11.—(1) A person need not comply with any request or order under section 7 to the extent that compliance would, by revealing evidence of the commission of any offence other than an offence under this Act, expose him to proceedings for that offence.

(2) Information disclosed by any person in compliance with any request or order under section 7 shall not be admissible against him in proceedings for an offence under this Act.

NOTES

[1]Words added by the Freedom of Information Act 2000 (c.36), Sched. 6, para. 6, effective May 14, 2001.

[2]As amended by the Northern Ireland Act 1998 (c.47), Sched. 13, para. 21(2), effective December 2, 1999.

[3]Words substituted by the Freedom of Information Act 2000 (c.36), Sched. 6, para. 7, effective May 14, 2001

GENERAL NOTE

Paragraph 1

Paragraph 1 exempts confidential references prepared by a data controller, in confidence, from the subject access provisions for the purposes set out in subparagraphs (a) to (c). The exemption will not apply if a person other than the data controller has prepared the confidential reference.

If a data subject requests access to a confidential reference which is held by the recipient of the reference, the recipient cannot claim the benefit of the exemption, but may be able to withhold disclosure under section 7(4) by the fact that the disclosure would reveal the identity of the referee. It is unlikely that a disclosure to the data subject under section 7(6) will be reasonable if the reference was given in confidence.

For example, if an employer holds in the employee's file a confidential reference from a previous employer, the current employer cannot rely on this exemption to avoid disclosing the reference to the employee. The current employer should first check with the previous employer that they have no objection to the contents of the reference being disclosed to the employee. If the previous employer objects the current employer should look to see if the reference can be disclosed without divulging the identity of the previous employer, or whether his identity can be blocked out. If the reference cannot be disclosed without making this information available to the employee, the current employer is not required to make the reference available to the employee.

Paragraph 1(c) covers individuals and organisations that provide confidential references about data subjects who carry on their own businesses.

Paragraph 2

Paragraph 2 relates to the armed forces and provides an exemption in respect of the subject information provisions. The exemption will only apply on a case-by-case basis and only when the particular circumstances mean that complying with the subject information provisions would be likely to prejudice the "combat effectiveness" of any of the Armed Forces. The exemption is qualified to provide safeguards for individuals. "Combat effectiveness" is not defined and may therefore be interpreted widely.

Paragraph 3

Paragraph 3 exempts personal data from the subject information provisions where they relate to judicial appointments and honours and this paragraph is most likely to be applied by the Lord Chancellor's department. The intention is to provide safeguards in assessing judicial appointments or removals and the conferring of honours by the Crown.

Paragraph 4

Paragraph 4 empowers the Secretary of State to make an order exempting from the subject information provisions personal data that are processed to assess whether a person is suitable for employment by or under the Crown or in an office appointed by the Queen, a Minister of the Crown or a Northern Ireland department. This paragraph will only take effect once the Secretary of State makes an order to this effect.

Paragraph 5

Paragraph 5 is an exemption that allows data controllers to plan their future management activities whilst preserving their confidentiality. This is a wide-ranging exemption but is subject to several conditions designed to protect data subjects.

Personal data processed for the purposes of "management forecasting" or "management planning" are exempt from the subject information provisions under this paragraph. Neither term is defined in the Act, but it is envisaged that the terms include the planning of redundancies, promotions, demotions, and other staffing matters, even possibly including an employer's intention to take disciplinary action against a particular employee. The "management forecasting" and "management planning" activities do not necessarily have to be related to the data controller's own business, but may be in respect of any business and any activity.

The exemption is qualified and can only be applied on a case-by-case basis, and only to such an extent that by complying with the subject information provisions, the business or other activity being carried out may be prejudiced.

Paragraph 6

Paragraph 6 contains an exemption that only applies where personal data are processed by a data controller for the purpose of providing a "corporate finance service" by a "relevant person" (defined in subparagraph (3)). Personal data are exempt from the subject access provisions on a case-by-case basis and only to the extent to which subject access could affect the price of any "instrument" (defined in subparagraph (3)). During the reading of the Data Protection Bill in the House of Lords, the Government explained the importance of this provision:

"The list rules of the London Stock Exchange require information to be disseminated to the market through its regulatory news service to ensure the orderly release of price sensitive information. Therefore, the rationale behind these safeguards is to prevent partial and unregulated dissemination of information from disrupting and corrupting the financial markets and the associated efficient allocation of capital in our economy."

Paragraph 7

Paragraph 7 contains a partial exemption from the subject information provisions in relation to personal data consisting of records of the data controller's intentions in respect of any negotiations that may be under way with the data subject. The exemption would be applied on a case-by-case basis. Negotiations may be in respect of pay increases, severance packages or redundancy payments. If applying the subject information provisions would be unlikely to prejudice the negotiations, this exemption cannot be relied upon. Possible future negotiations may also be covered by this paragraph. An example would be an insurance company recording on a customer's file how much it would be prepared to pay if a claim were settled in the future. Disclosure of that particular piece of information would harm any future negotiations.

It is unlikely that the exemption would apply in negotiations concerning the data subject between the data controller and a third party, as the provision specifically states that the negotiations should be "with the data subject".

Paragraph 8

Paragraph 8 provides an extension of the time limit in complying with a subject information request and is not an exemption as such. It applies in respect of examination marks or other information regarding examinations and is to prevent a data subject gaining access to his exam results before they have been officially announced. The meaning of "examination" includes any test to determine the knowledge, intelligence, skill or ability of the candidate.

Paragraph 9

Paragraph 9 provides an exemption from the subject information provisions in relation to a candidate's access to an examination script once it has been handed in for marking. Candidates do, however, have a right to certain information from the data controller, such as expressions of opinion about their performance in the examination if the opinion is recorded on the script and forms part of a relevant filing system. The meaning of "examination" includes any test to determine the knowledge, intelligence, skill or ability of the candidate.

Paragraph 10

Paragraph 10 provides an exemption from the subject information provisions in relation to information that is subject to a claim for legal professional privilege. An example is if a solicitor disclosed personal data relating to a third party in correspondence to a client, the third party would have no right of access to that correspondence. This privilege does not extend to members of other professions outwith the legal profession.

Paragraph 11

Paragraph 11 provides an exemption in two parts. First, a person is exempt from complying with a request or order for subject access if it would allow evidence about the commission of an offence by him to be revealed. This does not apply to evidence about an offence under this Act, however. The second part of the exemption states that information disclosed by any person under section 7 is inadmissible in proceedings for an offence under this Act.

Data Protection Act 1998

Section 39

TRANSITIONAL RELIEF

PART I

INTERPRETATION OF SCHEDULE

1.—(1) For the purposes of this Schedule, personal data are "eligible data" at any time if, and to the extent that, they are at that time subject to processing which was already under way immediately before 24th October 1998.

(2) In this Schedule—

"eligible automated data" means eligible data which fall within paragraph (a) or (b) of the definition of "data" in section 1(1);

"eligible manual data" means eligible data which are not eligible automated data;

"the first transitional period" means the period beginning with the commencement of this Schedule and ending with 23rd October 2001;

"the second transitional period" means the period beginning with 24th October 2001 and ending with 23rd October 2007.

GENERAL NOTE

This Schedule contains some transitional provisions with regard to the processing of automated and manual data that were already being processed prior to October 24, 1998. Processing which commenced after that date must immediately be carried out in compliance with the provisions of the Act and processing which was already under way prior to October 24, 1998 had three years, that is until October 23, 2001, to comply with the provisions of the Act.

From October 24, 2001, all automated processing of personal data was required to comply with the Act.

The transitional relief applied to manual data is more extensive and manual data that were already being processed prior to October 24, 1998 will still have limited exemptions until October 23, 2007.

Part I of the Schedule sets out definitions. The provisions apply to "eligible automated data" and "eligible manual data". "Eligible data" are data that have undergone processing prior to October 24, 1998.

The Information Commissioner's Guidelines discuss "processing already under way" and suggest that processing should be viewed in relation to the system as a whole and not to specific data sets relating to specific individuals. In the Information Commissioner's view, the addition of data to a system or the generation of data within a system should not be viewed as new processing. In this way, a new file created in respect of a new customer after October 24, 1998 (which should technically be viewed as new processing) will fall under the definition of "processing already under way" since the new file will fall within the existing operation for processing.

PART II

EXEMPTIONS AVAILABLE BEFORE 24TH OCTOBER 2001

Manual data

2.—(1) Eligible manual data, other than data forming part of an accessible record, are exempt from the data protection principles and Parts II and III of this Act during the first transitional period.

(2) This paragraph does not apply to eligible manual data to which paragraph 4 applies.

3.—(1) This paragraph applies to—

(a) eligible manual data forming part of an accessible record, and

(b) personal data which fall within paragraph (d) of the definition of "data" in section 1(1) but which, because they are not subject to processing which was already under way immediately before 24th October 1998, are not eligible data for the purposes of this Schedule.

(2) During the first transitional period, data to which this paragraph applies are exempt from—

(a) the data protection principles, except the sixth principle so far as relating to sections 7 and 12A,

(b) Part II of this Act, except—

(i) section 7 (as it has effect subject to section 8) and section 12A, and

(ii) section 15 so far as relating to those sections, and

(c) Part III of this Act.

4.—(1) This paragraph applies to eligible manual data which consist of information relevant to the financial standing of the data subject and in respect of which the data controller is a credit reference agency.

(2) During the first transitional period, data to which this paragraph applies are exempt from—

(a) the data protection principles, except the sixth principle so far as relating to sections 7 and 12A,

(b) Part II of this Act, except—

(i) section 7 (as it has effect subject to sections 8 and 9) and section 12A, and

(ii) section 15 so far as relating to those sections, and

(c) Part III of this Act.

Processing otherwise than by reference to the data subject

5. During the first transitional period, for the purposes of this Act (apart from paragraph 1), eligible automated data are not to be regarded as being "processed" unless the processing is by reference to the data subject.

Payrolls and accounts

6.—(1) Subject to sub-paragraph (2), eligible automated data processed by a data controller for one or more of the following purposes—

(a) calculating amounts payable by way of remuneration or pensions in respect of service in any employment or office or making payments of, or of sums deducted from, such remuneration or pensions, or

(b) keeping accounts relating to any business or other activity carried on by the data controller or keeping records of purchases, sales or other transactions for the purpose of ensuring that the requisite payments are made by or to him in respect of those transactions or for the purpose of making financial or management forecasts to assist him in the conduct of any such business or activity,

are exempt from the data protection principles and Parts II and III of this Act during the first transitional period.

(2) It shall be a condition of the exemption of any eligible automated data under this paragraph that the data are not processed for any other purpose, but the exemption is not lost by any processing of the eligible data for any other purpose if the data controller shows that he had taken such care to prevent it as in all the circumstances was reasonably required.

(3) Data processed only for one or more of the purposes mentioned in sub-paragraph (1)(a) may be disclosed—

(a) to any person, other than the data controller, by whom the remuneration or pensions in question are payable;

(b) for the purpose of obtaining actuarial advice,

(c) for the purpose of giving information as to the persons in any employment or office for use in medical research into the health of, or injuries suffered by, persons engaged in particular occupations or working in particular places or areas,

(d) if the data subject (or a person acting on his behalf) has requested or consented to the disclosure of the data either generally or in the circumstances in which the disclosure in question is made, or

(e) if the person making the disclosure has reasonable grounds for believing that the disclosure falls within paragraph (d).

(4) Data processed for any of the purposes mentioned in sub-paragraph (1) may be disclosed—

(a) for the purpose of audit or where the disclosure is for the purpose only of giving information about the data controller's financial affairs, or

(b) in any case in which disclosure would be permitted by any other provision of this Part of this Act if sub-paragraph (2) were included among the non-disclosure provisions.

(5) In this paragraph "remuneration" includes remuneration in kind and "pensions" includes gratuities or similar benefits.

Unincorporated members' clubs and mailing lists

7. Eligible automated data processed by an unincorporated members' club and relating only to the members of the club are exempt from the data protection principles and Parts II and III of this Act during the first transitional period.

8. Eligible automated data processed by a data controller only for the purposes of distributing, or recording the distribution of, articles or information to the data subjects and consisting only of their names, addresses or other particulars necessary for effecting the distribution, are exempt from the data protection principles and Parts II and III of this Act during the first transitional period.

9. Neither paragraph 7 nor paragraph 8 applies to personal data relating to any data subject unless he has been asked by the club or data controller whether he objects to the data relating to him being processed as mentioned in that paragraph and has not objected.

10. It shall be a condition of the exemption of any data under paragraph 7 that the data are not disclosed except as permitted by paragraph 11 and of the exemption under paragraph 8 that the data are not processed for any purpose other than that mentioned in that paragraph or as permitted by paragraph 11, but—
    (a) the exemption under paragraph 7 shall not be lost by any disclosure in breach of that condition, and
    (b) the exemption under paragraph 8 shall not be lost by any processing in breach of that condition,
if the data controller shows that he had taken such care to prevent it as in all the circumstances was reasonably required.

11. Data to which paragraph 10 applies may be disclosed—
    (a) if the data subject (or a person acting on his behalf) has requested or consented to the disclosure of the data either generally or in the circumstances in which the disclosure in question is made,
    (b) if the person making the disclosure has reasonable grounds for believing that the disclosure falls within paragraph (a), or
    (c) in any case in which disclosure would be permitted by any other provision of this Part of this Act if paragraph 8 were included among the non-disclosure provisions.

Back-up data

12. Eligible automated data which are processed only for the purpose of replacing other data in the event of the latter being lost, destroyed or impaired are exempt from section 7 during the first transitional period.

Exemption of all eligible automated data from certain requirements

13.—(1) During the first transitional period, eligible automated data are exempt from the following provisions—
    (a) the first data protection principle to the extent to which it requires compliance with—
      (i) paragraph 2 of Part II of Schedule 1,
      (ii) the conditions in Schedule 2, and
      (iii) the conditions in Schedule 3,
    (b) the seventh data protection principle to the extent to which it requires compliance with paragraph 12 of Part II of Schedule 1;
    (c) the eighth data protection principle,
    (d) in section 7(1), paragraphs (b), (c)(ii) and (d),
    (e) sections 10 and 11,
    (f) section 12, and
    (g) section 13, except so far as relating to—
      (i) any contravention of the fourth data protection principle,
      (ii) any disclosure without the consent of the data controller,
      (iii) loss or destruction of data without the consent of the data controller, or
      (iv) processing for the special purposes.
(2) The specific exemptions conferred by sub-paragraph (1)(a), (c) and (e) do not limit the data controller's general duty under the first data protection principle to ensure that processing is fair.

GENERAL NOTE

Part II sets out the exemptions that apply during the first transitional period (from October 24, 1998 until October 23, 2001).

Schedules

EXEMPTIONS AVAILABLE AFTER 23RD OCTOBER 2001 BUT BEFORE 24TH OCTOBER 2007

14.—(1) This paragraph applies to—
(a) eligible manual data which were held immediately before 24th October 1998, and
(b) personal data which fall within paragraph (d) of the definition of "data" in section 1(1) but do not fall within paragraph (a) of this sub-paragraph.
but does not apply to eligible manual data to which the exemption in paragraph 16 applies.
(2) During the second transitional period, data to which this paragraph applies are exempt from the following provisions—
(a) the first data protection principle except to the extent to which it requires compliance with paragraph 2 of Part II of Schedule 1,
(b) the second, third, fourth and fifth data protection principles, and
(c) section 14(1) to (3).

GENERAL NOTE
Part III sets out exemptions that apply during the second transitional period (from October 24, 2001 until October 23, 2007).

PART IV

EXEMPTIONS AFTER 23RD OCTOBER 2001 FOR HISTORICAL RESEARCH

15. In this Part of this Schedule "the relevant conditions" has the same meaning as in section 33.
16.—(1) Eligible manual data which are processed only for the purpose of historical research in compliance with the relevant conditions are exempt from the provisions specified in sub-paragraph (2) after 23rd October 2001.
(2) The provisions referred to in sub-paragraph (1) are—
(a) the first data protection principle except in so far as it requires compliance with paragraph 2 of Part II of Schedule 1,
(b) the second, third, fourth and fifth data protection principles, and
(c) section 14(1) to (3).
17.—(1) After 23rd October 2001 eligible automated data which are processed only for the purpose of historical research in compliance with the relevant conditions are exempt from the first data protection principle to the extent to which it requires compliance with the conditions in Schedules 2 and 3.
(2) Eligible automated data which are processed—
(a) only for the purpose of historical research,
(b) in compliance with the relevant conditions, and
(c) otherwise than by reference to the data subject,
are also exempt from the provisions referred to in sub-paragraph (3) after 23rd October 2001.
(3) The provisions referred to in sub-paragraph (2) are—
(a) the first data protection principle except in so far as it requires compliance with paragraph 2 of Part II of Schedule 1,
(b) the second, third, fourth and fifth data protection principles, and
(c) section 14(1) to (3).
18. For the purposes of this Part of this Schedule personal data are not to be treated as processed otherwise than for the purpose of historical research merely because the data are disclosed—
(a) to any person, for the purpose of historical research only,
(b) to the data subject or a person acting on his behalf,
(c) at the request, or with the consent, of the data subject or a person acting on his behalf, or
(d) in circumstances in which the person making the disclosure has reasonable grounds for believing that the disclosure falls within paragraph (a), (b) or (c).

GENERAL NOTE
Part IV sets out exemptions applying after the end of the first transitional period in relation to historical research.

PART V

EXEMPTION FROM SECTION 22

19. Processing which was already under way immediately before 24th October 1998 is not assessable processing for the purposes of section 22.

SCHEDULE 9

Section 50

POWERS OF ENTRY AND INSPECTION

Issue of warrants

1.—(1) If a circuit judge is satisfied by information on oath supplied by the Commissioner that there are reasonable grounds for suspecting—
   (a) that a data controller has contravened or is contravening any of the data protection principles, or
   (b) that an offence under this Act has been or is being committed,
and that evidence of the contravention or of the commission of the offence is to be found on any premises specified in the information, he may, subject to sub-paragraph (2) and paragraph 2 grant a warrant to the Commissioner.

(2) A judge shall not issue a warrant under this Schedule in respect of any personal data processed for the special purposes unless a determination by the Commissioner under section 45 with respect to those data has taken effect.

(3) A warrant issued under sub-paragraph (1) shall authorise the Commissioner or any of his officers or staff at any time within seven days of the date of the warrant to enter the premises, to search them, to inspect, examine, operate and test any equipment found there which is used or intended to be used for the processing of personal data and to inspect and seize any documents or other material found there which may be such evidence as is mentioned in that sub-paragraph.

2.—(1) A judge shall not issue a warrant under this Schedule unless he is satisfied—
   (a) that the Commissioner has given seven days' notice in writing to the occupier of the premises in question demanding access to the premises, and
   (b) that either—
      (i) access was demanded at a reasonable hour and was unreasonably refused, or
      (ii) although entry to the premises was granted, the occupier unreasonably refused to comply with a request by the Commissioner or any of the Commissioner's officers or staff to permit the Commissioner or the officer or member of staff to do any of the things referred to in paragraph 1(3), and
   (c) that the occupier, has, after the refusal, been notified by the Commissioner of the application for the warrant and has had an opportunity of being heard by the judge on the question whether or not it should be issued.

(2) Sub-paragraph (1) shall not apply if the judge is satisfied that the case is one of urgency or that compliance with those provisions would defeat the object of the entry.

3. A judge who issues a warrant under this Schedule shall also issue two copies of it and certify them clearly as copies.

Execution of warrants

4. A person executing a warrant issued under this Schedule may use such reasonable force as may be necessary.

5. A warrant issued under this Schedule shall be executed at a reasonable hour unless it appears to the person executing it that there are grounds for suspecting that the evidence in question would not be found if it were so executed.

6. If the person who occupies the premises in respect of which a warrant is issued under this Schedule is present when the warrant is executed, he shall be shown the warrant and supplied with a copy of it; and if that person is not present a copy of the warrant shall be left in a prominent place on the premises.

7.—(1) A person seizing anything in pursuance of a warrant under this Schedule shall give a receipt for it if asked to do so.

(2) Anything so seized may be retained for so long as is necessary in all the circumstances but the person in occupation of the premises in question shall be given a copy of anything that is seized if he so requests and the person executing the warrant considers that it can be done without undue delay.

Matters exempt from inspection and seizure

8. The powers of inspection and seizure conferred by a warrant issued under this Schedule shall not be exercisable in respect of personal data which by virtue of section 28 are exempt from any of the provisions of this Act.

9.—(1) Subject to the provisions of this paragraph, the powers of inspection and seizure conferred by a warrant issued under this Schedule shall not be exercisable in respect of—

(a) any communication between a professional legal adviser and his client in connection with the giving of legal advice to the client with respect to his obligations, liabilities or rights under this Act, or

(b) any communication between a professional legal adviser and his client, or between such an adviser or his client and any other person, made in connection with or in contemplation of proceedings under or arising out of this Act (including proceedings before the Tribunal) and for the purposes of such proceedings.

(2) Sub-paragraph (1) applies also to—

(a) any copy or other record of any such communication as is there mentioned, and

(b) any document or article enclosed with or referred to in any such communication if made in connection with the giving of any advice or, as the case may be, in connection with or in contemplation of and for the purposes of such proceedings as are there mentioned.

(3) This paragraph does not apply to anything in the possession of any person other than the professional legal adviser or his client or to anything held with the intention of furthering a criminal purpose.

(4) In this paragraph references to the client of a professional legal adviser include references to any person representing such a client.

10. If the person in occupation of any premises in respect of which a warrant is issued under this Schedule objects to the inspection or seizure under the warrant of any material on the grounds that it consists partly of matters in respect of which those powers are not exercisable, he shall, if the person executing the warrant so requests, furnish that person with a copy of so much of the material as is not exempt from those powers.

Return of warrants

11. A warrant issued under this Schedule shall be returned to the court from which it was issued—

(a) after being executed, or

(b) if not executed within the time authorised for its execution;

and the person by whom any such warrant is executed shall make an endorsement on it stating what powers have been exercised by him under the warrant.

Offences

12. Any person who—

(a) intentionally obstructs a person in the execution of a warrant issued under this Schedule, or

(b) fails without reasonable excuse to give any person executing such a warrant such assistance as he may reasonably require for the execution of the warrant,

is guilty of an offence.

Vessels, vehicles etc.

13. In this Schedule "premises" includes any vessel, vehicle, aircraft or hovercraft, and references to the occupier of any premises include references to the person in charge of any vessel, vehicle, aircraft or hovercraft.

Scotland and Northern Ireland

14. In the application of this Schedule to Scotland—

(a) for any reference to a circuit judge there is substituted a reference to the sheriff,

(b) for any reference to information on oath there is substituted a reference to evidence on oath, and

(c) for the reference to the court from which the warrant was issued there is substituted a reference to the sheriff clerk.

15. In the application of this Schedule to Northern Ireland—

(a) for any reference to a circuit judge there is substituted a reference to a county court judge, and

(b) for any reference to information on oath there is substituted a reference to a complaint on oath.

GENERAL NOTE

Section 50 gives effect to this Schedule that deals with the Information Commissioner's powers of entry and inspection and sets out the procedures to be followed.

A judge may grant a warrant to allow the Information Commissioner to take entry and to inspect premises. The warrant will only be issued if the judge determines that there are reasonable grounds for suspicion of an offence having been committed or the data protection principles having been breached. The information from the Information Commissioner justifying the granting of the warrant has to be given on oath and may be attached to the warrant, similar to the practice on the granting of police warrants. The powers under a warrant are wide. Any member of the Information Commissioner's staff is able to exercise the powers under the warrant.

The warrant should state the address of the premises, although the premises do not necessarily need to be the place of business of the data controller. It is more likely that the specified premises will be the place where the processing is carried out, such as the address of the data processor if one is involved.

Only if the Information Commissioner has made a determination under section 45 will the judge issue a warrant relating to the processing of personal data for the special purposes (sections 13, 32 and 44). This avoids the media being exposed to litigation for data protection reasons prior to publication. In these circumstances, the Information Commissioner's powers are deferred until such time as a determination under section 45 can be made.

The judge must be satisfied before issuing a warrant that the Information Commissioner has served notice requesting access to the premises in writing on the occupier of the premises at least seven days prior to the application for the grant of a warrant. In addition, the Information Commissioner must have previously requested access at a reasonable hour (presumably normal office hours) which was unreasonably denied, or alternatively access was granted but the occupier unreasonably refused to comply with the Information Commissioner's request (paragraph 2).

Only if the judge is satisfied that there is urgency in the matter will he dispense with the period of notice and issue the warrant immediately.

The Information Commissioner is unable to exercise powers of entry and inspection in relation to personal data that is exempt under section 28 (the national security exemption) and also between legal advisers and clients (sections 9(2), 9(3) and 10). If such personal data is taken under the warrant, the powers under the warrant are exceeded and the evidence obtained will be deemed inadmissible. It may prove difficult to distinguish at the searching stage as to what information is exempt and what is not.

Paragraph 12 creates offences with regard to obstruction of the execution of a warrant and failure to assist in the execution of the warrant, and these offences are triable summarily, with the maximum penalty being a fine not exceeding level 5 of the statutory maximum (see section 60(3)).

Where a warrant is not granted under this Schedule, the Information Commissioner may be able to exercise other powers, such as the issuing of an information notice (section 49) or an enforcement notice (section 40).

SCHEDULE 10

Section 53(6)

FURTHER PROVISIONS RELATING TO ASSISTANCE UNDER SECTION 53

1. In this Schedule "applicant" and "proceedings" have the same meaning as in section 53.

2. The assistance provided under section 53 may include the making of arrangements for, or for the Commissioner to bear the costs of—

(a) the giving of advice or assistance by a solicitor or counsel, and

Schedules

(b) the representation of the applicant, or the provision to him of such assistance as is usually given by a solicitor or counsel—

(i) in steps preliminary or incidental to the proceedings, or

(ii) in arriving at or giving effect to a compromise to avoid or bring an end to the proceedings.

3. Where assistance is provided with respect to the conduct of proceedings—

(a) it shall include an agreement by the Commissioner to indemnify the applicant (subject only to any exceptions specified in the notification) in respect of any liability to pay costs or expenses arising by virtue of any judgment or order of the court in the proceedings,

(b) it may include an agreement by the Commissioner to indemnify the applicant in respect of any liability to pay costs or expenses arising by virtue of any compromise or settlement arrived at in order to avoid the proceedings or bring the proceedings to an end, and

(c) it may include an agreement by the Commissioner to indemnify the applicant in respect of any liability to pay damages pursuant to an undertaking given on the grant of interlocutory relief (in Scotland, an interim order) to the applicant.

4. Where the Commissioner provides assistance in relation to any proceedings, he shall do so on such terms, or make such other arrangements, as will secure that a person against whom the proceedings have been or are commenced is informed that assistance has been or is being provided by the Commissioner in relation to them.

5. In England and Wales or Northern Ireland, the recovery of expenses incurred by the Commissioner in providing an applicant with assistance (as taxed or assessed in such manner as may be prescribed by rules of court) shall constitute a first charge for the benefit of the Commissioner—

(a) on any costs which, by virtue of any judgment or order of the court, are payable to the applicant by any other person in respect of the matter in connection with which the assistance is provided, and

(b) on any sum payable to the applicant under a compromise or settlement arrived at in connection with that matter to avoid or bring to an end any proceedings.

6. In Scotland, the recovery of such expenses (as taxed or assessed in such manner as may be prescribed by rules of court) shall be paid to the Commissioner, in priority to other debts—

(a) out of any expenses which, by virtue of any judgment or order of the court, are payable to the applicant by any other person in respect of the matter in connection with which the assistance is provided, and

(b) out of any sum payable to the applicant under a compromise or settlement arrived at in connection with that matter to avoid or bring to an end any proceedings.

GENERAL NOTE

In cases of substantial public importance, the Information Commissioner may provide assistance to an individual in relation to legal proceedings connected to processing for one of the special purposes. The aim of these provisions is to ensure that cases of substantial public importance are determined and do not remain undecided due to a lack of resources on the part of the applicant (*i.e.* the pursuer or plaintiff). This Schedule sets out the assistance that the Information Commissioner may provide an individual.

The individual will be indemnified by the Information Commissioner in respect of any liability for costs and expenses incurred as a result of the judgment of the court. The Information Commissioner can decide whether to meet any expenses and costs incurred prior to reaching a settlement between the parties.

Paragraphs 5 and 6 provide that the Information Commissioner is entitled to a reimbursement of expenses by the applicant from any damages or settlement received by the applicant. However, the Information Commissioner is not entitled to claim any sums from an award of compensation under section 13 of the Act.

SCHEDULE 11

Section 68(1)(b)

EDUCATIONAL RECORDS

Meaning of "educational record"

1. For the purposes of section 68 "educational record" means any record to which paragraph 2, 5 or 7 applies.

England and Wales

2. This paragraph applies to any record of information which—

(a) is processed by or on behalf of the governing body of, or a teacher at, any school in England and Wales specified in paragraph 3,

(b) relates to any person who is or has been a pupil at the school, and

(c) originated from or was supplied by or on behalf of any of the persons specified in paragraph 4,

other than information which is processed by a teacher solely for the teacher's own use.

3. The schools referred to in paragraph 2(a) are—

(a) a school maintained by a local education authority, and

(b) a special school, as defined by section 6(2) of the Education Act 1996, which is not so maintained.

4. The persons referred to in paragraph 2(c) are—

(a) an employee of the local education authority which maintains the school,

(b) in the case of—

   (i) a voluntary aided, foundation or foundation special school (within the meaning of the School Standards and Framework Act 1998), or

   (ii) a special school which is not maintained by a local education authority,

   a teacher or other employee at the school (including an educational psychologist engaged by the governing body under a contract for services),

(c) the pupil to whom the record relates, and

(d) a parent, as defined by section 576(1) of the Education Act 1996, of that pupil.

Scotland

5. This paragraph applies to any record of information which is processed—

(a) by an education authority in Scotland, and

(b) for the purpose of the relevant function of the authority,

other than information which is processed by a teacher solely for the teacher's own use.

6. For the purposes of paragraph 5—

(a) "education authority" means an education authority within the meaning of the Education (Scotland) Act 1980 ("the 1980 Act") or, in relation to a self-governing school, the board of management within the meaning of the Self-Governing Schools etc. (Scotland) Act 1989 ("the 1989 Act"),

(b) "the relevant function" means, in relation to each of those authorities, their function under section 1 of the 1980 Act and section 7(1) of the 1989 Act, and

(c) information processed by an education authority is processed for the purpose of the relevant function of the authority if the processing relates to the discharge of that function in respect of a person—

   (i) who is or has been a pupil in a school provided by the authority, or

   (ii) who receives, or has received, further education (within the meaning of the 1980 Act) so provided.

Northern Ireland

7.—(1) This paragraph applies to any record of information which—

(a) is processed by or on behalf of the Board of Governors of, or a teacher at, any grant-aided school in Northern Ireland,

(b) relates to any person who is or has been a pupil at the school, and

(c) originated from or was supplied by or on behalf of any of the persons specified in paragraph 8,

other than information which is processed by a teacher solely for the teacher's own use.

(2) In sub-paragraph (1) "grant-aided school" has the same meaning as in the Education and Libraries (Northern Ireland) Order 1986.

8. The persons referred to in paragraph 7(1) are—

(a) a teacher at the school,

(b) an employee of an education and library board, other than such a teacher,

(c) the pupil to whom the record relates, and

(d) a parent (as defined by Article 2(2) of the Education and Libraries (Northern Ireland) Order 1986) of that pupil.

Schedules

England and Wales: transitory provisions

9.—(1) Until the appointed day within the meaning of section 20 of the School Standards and Framework Act 1998, this Schedule shall have effect subject to the following modifications.

(2) Paragraph 3 shall have effect as if for paragraph (b) and the "and" immediately preceding it there were substituted—

"(aa) a grant-maintained school, as defined by section 183(1) of the Education Act 1996,

(ab) a grant-maintained special school, as defined by section 337(4) of that Act, and

(b) a special school, as defined by section 6(2) of that Act, which is neither a maintained special school, as defined by section 337(3) of that Act, nor a grant-maintained special school."

(3) Paragraph 4(b)(i) shall have effect as if for the words from "foundation", in the first place where it occurs, to "1998)" there were substituted "or grant-maintained school".

SCHEDULE 12

Section 68(1)(c)

ACCESSIBLE PUBLIC RECORDS

Meaning of "accessible public record"

1. For the purposes of section 68 "accessible public record" means any record which is kept by an authority specified—

(a) as respects England and Wales, in the Table in paragraph 2,

(b) as respects Scotland, in the Table in paragraph 4, or

(c) as respects Northern Ireland, in the Table in paragraph 6,

and is a record of information of a description specified in that Table in relation to that authority.

Housing and social services records: England and Wales

2. The following is the Table referred to in paragraph 1(a).

TABLE OF AUTHORITIES AND INFORMATION

The authorities	*The accessible information*
Housing Act local authority.	Information held for the purpose of any of the authority's tenancies.
Local social services authority.	Information held for any purpose of the authority's social services functions.

3.—(1) The following provisions apply for the interpretation of the Table in paragraph 2.

(2) Any authority which, by virtue of section 4(e) of the Housing Act 1985, is a local authority for the purpose of any provision of that Act is a "Housing Act local authority" for the purposes of this Schedule, and so is any housing action trust established under Part III of the Housing Act 1988.

(3) Information contained in records kept by a Housing Act local authority is "held for the purpose of any of the authority's tenancies" if it is held for any purpose of the relationship of landlord and tenant of a dwelling which subsists, has substituted or may subsist between the authority and any individual who is, has been or, as the case may be, has applied to be, a tenant of the authority.

(4) Any authority which, by virtue of section 1 or 12 of the Local Authority Social Services Act 1970, is or is treated as a local authority for the purposes of that Act is a "local social services authority" for the purposes of this Schedule; and information contained in records kept by such an authority is "held for any purpose of the authority's social services functions" if it is held for the purpose of any past, current or proposed exercise of such a function in any case.

(5) Any expression used in paragraph 2 or this paragraph and in Part II of the Housing Act 1985 or the Local Authority Social Services Act 1970 has the same meaning as in that Act.

Data Protection Act 1998

Housing and social services records: Scotland

4. The following is the Table referred to in paragraph 1(b).

TABLE OF AUTHORITIES AND INFORMATION

The authorities	*The accessible information*
Local authority. Scottish Homes. Social work authority.	Information held for the purpose of any of the body's tenancies. Information held for any purpose of the authority's functions under the Social Work (Scotland) Act 1968 and the enactments referred to in section 5(1B) of that Act.

5.—(1) The following provisions apply for the interpretation of the Table in paragraph 4.

(2) "Local authority" means —

(a) a council constituted under section 2 of the Local Government etc. (Scotland) Act 1994,

(b) a joint board or joint committee of two or more of those councils, or

(c) any trust under the control of such a council.

(3) Information contained in records kept by a local authority or Scottish Homes is held for the purpose of any of their tenancies if it is held for any purpose of the relationship of landlord and tenant of a dwelling-house which subsists, has subsisted or may subsist between the authority or, as the case may be, Scottish Homes and any individual who is, has been or, as the case may be, has applied to be a tenant of theirs.

(4) "Social work authority" means a local authority for the purposes of the Social Work (Scotland) Act 1968; and information contained in records kept by such an authority is held for any purpose of their functions if it is held for the purpose of any past, current or proposed exercise of such a function in any case.

Housing and social services records: Northern Ireland

6. The following is the Table referred to in paragraph 1(c).

TABLE OF AUTHORITIES AND INFORMATION

The authorities	*The accessible information*
The Northern Ireland Housing Executive.	Information held for the purpose of any of the Executive's tenancies.
A Health and Social Services Board.	Information held for the purpose of any past, current or proposed exercise by the Board of any function exercisable, by virtue of directions under Article 17(1) of the Health and Personal Social Services (Northern Ireland) Order 1972, by the Board on behalf of the Department of Health and Social Services with respect to the administration of personal social services under— (a) the Children and Young Persons Act (Northern Ireland) 1968; (b) the Health and Personal Social Services (Northern Ireland) Order 1972; (c) Article 47 of the Matrimonial Causes (Northern Ireland) Order 1978; (d) Article 11 of the Domestic Proceedings (Northern Ireland) Order 1980;

	(e) the Adoption (Northern Ireland) Order 1987; or
	(f) the Children (Northern Ireland) Order 1995.
An HSS trust.	Information held for the purpose of any past, current or proposed exercise by the trust of any function exercisable, by virtue of an authorisation under Article 3(1) of the Health and Personal Social Services (Northern Ireland) Order 1994, by the trust on behalf of a Health and Social Services Board with respect to the administration of personal social services under any statutory provision mentioned in the last preceding entry.

7.—(1) This paragraph applies for the interpretation of the Table in paragraph 6,

(2) Information contained in records kept by the Northern Ireland Housing Executive is "held for the purpose of any of the Executive's tenancies" if it is held for any purpose of the relationship of landlord and tenant of a dwelling which subsists, has subsisted or may subsist between the Executive and any individual who is, has been or, as the case may be, has applied to be, a tenant of the Executive.

SCHEDULE 13

Section 72

MODIFICATIONS OF ACT HAVING EFFECT BEFORE 24TH OCTOBER 2007

1. After section 12 there is inserted—

"Rights of data subjects in relation to exempt manual data

12A.—(1) A data subject is entitled at any time by notice in writing—

(a) to require the data controller to rectify, block, erase or destroy exempt manual data which are inaccurate or incomplete, or

(b) to require the data controller to cease holding exempt manual data in a way incompatible with the legitimate purposes pursued by the data controller.

(2) A notice under subsection (1)(a) or (b) must state the data subject's reasons for believing that the data are inaccurate "or incomplete or, as the case may be, his reasons for believing that they are held in a way incompatible with the legitimate purposes pursued by the data controller.

(3) If the court is satisfied, on the application of any person who has given a notice under subsection (1) which appears to the court to be justified (or to be justified to any extent) that the data controller in question has failed to comply with the notice, the court may order him to take such steps for complying with the notice (or for complying with it to that extent) as the court thinks fit.

(4) In this section "exempt manual data" means —

(a) in relation to the first transitional period, as defined by paragraph 1(2) of Schedule 8, data to which paragraph 3 or 4 of that Schedule applies, and

(b) in relation to the second transitional period, as so defined, data to which paragraph 14 of that Schedule applies.

(5) For the purposes of this section personal data are incomplete if, and only if, the data, although not inaccurate, are such that their incompleteness would constitute a contravention of the third or fourth data protection principles, if those principles applied to the data."

2. In section 32—

(a) in subsection (2) after " section 12" there is inserted—

"(dd) section 12A,", and

(b) in subsection (4) after "12(8)" there is inserted ", 12A(3)".

3. In section 34 for " section 14(1) to (3)" there is substituted " sections 12A and 14(1) to (3)."

4. In section 53(1) after "12(8)" there is inserted ", 12A(3)".

5. In paragraph 8 of Part II of Schedule 1, the word "or" at the end of paragraph (c) is omitted and after paragraph (d) there is inserted "or
    (e) he contravenes section 12A by failing to comply with a notice given under subsection (1) of that section to the extent that the notice is justified."

SCHEDULE 14

Section 73

TRANSITIONAL PROVISIONS AND SAVINGS

Interpretation

1. In this Schedule—
"the 1984 Act" means the Data Protection Act 1984;
"the old principles" means the data protection principles within the meaning of the 1984 Act;
"the new principles" means the data protection principles within the meaning of this Act.

Effect of registration under Part II of 1984 Act

2.—(1) Subject to sub-paragraphs (4) and (5) any person who, immediately before the commencement of Part III of this Act—
    (a) is registered as a data user under Part II of the 1984 Act, or
    (b) is treated by virtue of section 7(6) of the 1984 Act as so registered,
is exempt from section 17(1) of this Act until the end of the registration period[...]'.
    (2) In sub-paragraph (1) "the registration period", in relation to a person, means —
    (a) where there is a single entry in respect of that person as a data user, the period at the end of which, if section 8 of the 1984 Act had remained in force, that entry would have fallen to be removed unless renewed, and
    (b) where there are two or more entries in respect of that person as a data user, the period at the end of which, if that section had remained in force, the last of those entries to expire would have fallen to be removed unless renewed.
    (3) Any application for registration as a data user under Part II of the 1984 Act which is received by the Commissioner before the commencement of Part III of this Act (including any appeal against a refusal of registration) shall be determined in accordance with the old principles and the provisions of the 1984 Act.
    (4) If a person falling within paragraph (b) of sub-paragraph (1) receives a notification under section 7(1) of the 1984 Act of the refusal of his application, sub-paragraph (1) shall cease to apply to him—
    (a) if no appeal is brought, at the end of the period within which an appeal can be brought against the refusal, or
    (b) on the withdrawal or dismissal of the appeal.
    (5) If a data controller gives a notification under section 18(1) at a time when he is exempt from section 17(1) by virtue of sub-paragraph (1), he shall cease to be so exempt.
    (6) The Commissioner shall include in the register maintained under section 19 an entry in respect of each person who is exempt from section 17(1) by virtue of sub-paragraph (1); and each entry shall consist of the particulars which, immediately before the commencement of Part III of this Act, were included (or treated as included) in respect of that person in the register maintained under section 4 of the1984 Act.
    (7) Notification regulations under Part III of this Act may make provision modifying the duty referred to in section 20(1) in its application to any person in respect of whom an entry in the register maintained under section 19 has been made under sub-paragraph (6).
    (8) Notification regulations under Part III of this Act may make further transitional provision in connection with the substitution of Part III of this Act for Part II of the 1984 Act (registration), including provision modifying the application of provisions of Part III in transitional cases.

Rights of data subjects

3.—(1) The repeal of section 21 of the 1984 Act (right of access to personal data) does not affect the application of that section in any case in which the request (together with the information referred to in paragraph (a) of subsection (4) of that section and, in a case where it is required, the consent referred to in paragraph (b) of that subsection) was received before the day on which the repeal comes into force.

(2) Sub-paragraph (1) does not apply where the request is made by reference to this Act.

(3) Any fee paid for the purposes of section 21 of the 1984 Act before the commencement of section 7 in a case not falling within sub-paragraph (1) shall be taken to have been paid for the purposes of section 7.

4. The repeal of section 22 of the 1984 Act (compensation for inaccuracy) and the repeal of section 23 of that Act (compensation for loss or unauthorised disclosure) do not affect the application of those sections in relation to damage or distress suffered at any time by reason of anything done or omitted to be done before the commencement of the repeals.

5. The repeal of section 24 of the 1984 Act (rectification and erasure) does not affect any case in which the application to the court was made before the day on which the repeal comes into force.

6. Subsection (3)(b) of section 14 does not apply where the rectification, blocking, erasure or destruction occurred before the commencement of that section.

Enforcement and transfer prohibition notices served under Part V of 1984 Act

7.—(1) If, immediately before the commencement of section 40—
(a) an enforcement notice under section 10 of the 1984 Act has effect, and
(b) either the time for appealing against the notice has expired or any appeal has been determined,
then, after that commencement, to the extent mentioned in sub-paragraph (3), the notice shall have effect for the purposes of sections 41 and 47 as if it were an enforcement notice under section 40.

(2) Where an enforcement notice has been served under section 10 of the 1984 Act before the commencement of section 40 and immediately before that commencement either—
(a) the time for appealing against the notice has not expired, or
(b) an appeal has not been determined,
the appeal shall be determined in accordance with the provisions of the 1984 Act and the old principles and, unless the notice is quashed on appeal, to the extent mentioned in sub-paragraph (3) the notice shall have effect for the purposes of sections 41 and 47 as if it were an enforcement notice under section 40.

(3) An enforcement notice under section 10 of the 1984 Act has the effect described in sub-paragraph (1) or (2) only to the extent that the steps specified in the notice for complying with the old principles or principles in question are steps which the data controller could be required by an enforcement notice under section 40 to take for complying with the new principles or any of them.

8.—(1) If, immediately before the commencement of section 40—
(a) a transfer prohibition notice under section 12 of the 1984 Act has effect, and
(b) either the time for appealing against the notice has expired or any appeal has been determined,
then, on and after that commencement, to the extent specified in sub-paragraph (3), the notice shall have effect for the purposes of sections 41 and 47 as if it were an enforcement notice under section 40.

(2) Where a transfer prohibition notice has been served under section 12 of the 1984 Act and immediately before the commencement of section 40 either—
(a) the time for appealing against the notice has not expired, or
(b) an appeal has not been determined,
the appeal shall be determined in accordance with the provisions of the 1984 Act and the old principles and, unless the notice is quashed on appeal, to the extent mentioned in sub-paragraph (3) the notice shall have effect for the purposes of sections 41 and 47 as if it were an enforcement notice under section 40.

(3) A transfer prohibition notice under section 12 of the 1984 Act has the effect described in sub-paragraph (1) or (2) only to the extent that the prohibition imposed by the notice is one which could be imposed by an enforcement notice under section 40 for complying with the new principles or any of them.

Notices under new law relating to matters in relation to which 1984 Act had effect

9. The Commissioner may serve an enforcement notice under section 40 on or after the day on which that section comes into force if he is satisfied that, before that day, the data controller contravened the old principles by reason of any act or omission which would also have constituted a contravention of the new principles if they had applied before that day.

10. Subsection (5)(b) of section 40 does not apply where the rectification, blocking, erasure or destruction occurred before the commencement of that section.

11. The Commissioner may serve an information notice under section 43 on or after the day on which that section comes into force if he has reasonable grounds for suspecting that, before that day, the data controller contravened the old principles by reason of any act or omission which would also have constituted a contravention of the new principles if they had applied before that day.

12. Where by virtue of paragraph 11 an information notice is served on the basis of anything done or omitted to be done before the day on which section 43 comes into force, subsection (2)(b) of that section shall have effect as if the reference to the data controller having complied, or complying, with the new principles were a reference to the data controller having contravened the old principles by reason of any such act or omission as is mentioned in paragraph 11.

Self-incrimination, etc.

13.—(1) In section 43(8), section 44(9) and paragraph 11 of Schedule 7, any reference to an offence under this Act includes a reference to an offence under the 1984 Act.

(2) In section 34(9) of the 1984 Act, any reference to an offence under that Act includes a reference to an offence under this Act.

Warrants issued under 1984 Act

14. The repeal of Schedule 4 to the 1984 Act does not affect the application of that Schedule in any case where a warrant was issued under that Schedule before the commencement of the repeal.

Complaints under section 36(2) of 1984 Act and requests for assessment under section 42

15. The repeal of section 36(2) of the 1984 Act does not affect the application of that provision in any case where the complaint was received by the Commissioner before the commencement of the repeal.

16. In dealing with a complaint under section 36(2) of the 1984 Act or a request for an assessment under section 42 of this Act, the Commissioner shall have regard to the provisions from time to time applicable to the processing, and accordingly—

(a) in section 36(2) of the 1984 Act, the reference to the old principles and the provisions of that Act includes, in relation to any time when the new principles and the provisions of this Act have effect, those principles and provisions, and

(b) in section 42 of this Act, the reference to the provisions of this Act includes, in relation to any time when the old principles and the provisions of the 1984 Act had effect, those principles and provisions.

Applications under Access to Health Records Act 1990 or corresponding Northern Ireland legislation

17.—(1) The repeal of any provision of the Access to Health Records Act 1990 does not affect—

(a) the application of section 3 or 6 of that Act in any case in which the application under that section was received before the day on which the repeal comes into force, or

(b) the application of section 8 of that Act in any case in which the application to the court was made before the day on which the repeal comes into force.

(2) Sub-paragraph (1)(a) does not apply in relation to an application for access to information which was made by reference to this Act.

18.—(1) The revocation of any provision of the Access to Health Records (Northern Ireland) Order 1993 does not affect—

(a) the application of Article 5 or 8 of that Order in any case in which the application under that Article was received before the day on which the repeal comes into force, or

(b) the application of Article 10 of that Order in any case in which the application to the court was made before the day on which the repeal comes into force.

(2) Sub-paragraph (1)(a) does not apply in relation to an application for access to information which was made by reference to this Act.

Schedules

Applications under regulations under Access to Personal Files Act 1987 or corresponding Northern Ireland legislation

19.—(1) The repeal of the personal files enactments does not affect the application of regulations under those enactments in relation to—

(a) any request for information,

(b) any application for rectification or erasure, or

(c) any application for review of a decision,

which was made before the day on which the repeal comes into force.

(2) Sub-paragraph (1)(a) does not apply in relation to a request for information which was made by reference to this Act.

(3) In sub-paragraph (1) "the personal files enactments" means —

(a) in relation to Great Britain, the Access to Personal Files Act 1987, and

(b) in relation to Northern Ireland, Part II of the Access to Personal Files and Medical Reports (Northern Ireland) Order 1991.

Applications under section 158 of Consumer Credit Act 1974

20. Section 62 does not affect the application of section 158 of the Consumer Credit Act 1974 in any case where the request was received before the commencement of section 62, unless the request is made by reference to this Act.

NOTES

¹Words repealed by the Freedom of Information Act 2000 (c.36), Sched. 8, para. 1.

SCHEDULE 15

Section 74(1)

MINOR AND CONSEQUENTIAL AMENDMENTS

Public Records Act 1958 (c. 51)

1.—(1) *Repealed by the Freedom of Information Act 2000 (c.36), Sched. 8, para. 1.*

(2) That Schedule shall continue to have effect with the following amendment (originally made by paragraph 14 of Schedule 2 to the Data Protection Act 1984).

(3) After paragraph 4(1)(n) there is inserted—

"(nn) records of the Data Protection Tribunal".

Parliamentary Commissioner Act 1967 (c. 13)

2. *Repealed by the Freedom of Information Act 2000 (c.36), Sched. 8, para. 1.*

3. In Schedule 4 to that Act (tribunals exercising administrative functions), in the entry relating to the Data Protection Tribunal, for "section 3 of the Data Protection Act 1984" there is substituted "section 6 of the Data Protection Act 1998".

Superannuation Act 1972 (c. 11)

4. *Repealed by the Freedom of Information Act 2000 (c.36), Sched. 8, para. 1.*

House of Commons Disqualification Act 1975 (c. 24)

5.—(1) Part II of Schedule 1 to the House of Commons Disqualification Act 1975 (bodies whose members are disqualified) shall continue to include the entry "The Data Protection Tribunal" (originally inserted by paragraph 12(1) of Schedule 2 to the Data Protection Act 1984).

(2) *Repealed by the Freedom of Information Act 2000 (c.36), Sched. 8, para. 1.*

6.—(1) Part II of Schedule 1 to the Northern Ireland Assembly Disqualification Act 1975 (bodies whose members are disqualified) shall continue to include the entry "The Data Protection Tribunal" (originally inserted by paragraph 12(3) of Schedule 2 to the Data Protection Act 1984).

(2) *Repealed by the Freedom of Information Act 2000 (c.36), Sched. 8, para. 1.*

Representation of the People Act 1983 (c. 2)

7. In Schedule 2 of the Representation of the People Act 1983 (provisions which may be included in regulations as to registration etc), in paragraph 11A(2)—
   (a) for "data user" there is substituted "data controller", and
   (b) for "the Data Protection Act 1984" there is substituted "the Data Protection Act 1998".

Access to Medical Reports Act 1988 (c. 28)

8. In section 2(1) of the Access to Medical Reports Act 1988 (interpretation), in the definition of "health professional", for "the Data Protection (Subject Access Modification) Order 1987" there is substituted "the Data Protection Act 1998".

Football Spectators Act 1989 (c. 37)

9.—(1) Section 5 of the Football Spectators Act 1989 (national membership scheme; contents and penalties) is amended as follows.

(2) In subsection (5), for " paragraph 1(2) of Part II of Schedule 1 to the Data Protection Act 1984" there is substituted " paragraph 1(2) of Part II of Schedule 1 to the Data Protection Act 1998".

(3) In subsection (6), for " section 28(1) and (2) of the Data Protection Act 1984" there is substituted " section 29(1) and (2) of the Data Protection Act 1998".

Education (Student Loans) Act 1990 (c. 6)

10. Schedule 2 to the Education (Student Loans) Act 1990 (loans for students) so far as that Schedule continues in force shall have effect as if the reference in paragraph 4(2) to the Data Protection Act 1984 were a reference to this Act.

Access to Health Records Act 1990 (c. 23)

11. For section 2 of the Access to Health Records Act 1990 there is substituted—
"Health professionals
2. In this Act "health professional" has the same meaning as in the Data Protection Act 1998."
12. In section 3(4) of that Act (cases where fee may be required) in paragraph (a), for "the maximum prescribed under section 21 of the Data Protection Act 1984" there is substituted "such maximum as may be prescribed for the purposes of this section by regulations under section 7 of the Data Protection Act 1998".
13. In section 5(3) of that Act (cases where right of access may be partially excluded) for the words from the beginning to "record" in the first place where it occurs there is substituted "Access shall not be given under section 3(2) to any part of a health record".

Access to Personal Files and Medical Reports (Northern Ireland) Order 1991 (1991/1707 (N.I. 14))

14. In Article 4 of the Access to Personal Files and Medical Reports (Northern Ireland) Order 1991 (obligation to give access), in paragraph (2) (exclusion of information to which individual entitled under section 21 of the Data Protection Act 1984) for " section 21 of the Data Protection Act 1984" there is substituted " section 7 of the Data Protection Act 1998".
15. In Article 6(1) of that Order (interpretation), in the definition of "health professional", for "the Data Protection (Subject Access Modification) (Health) Order 1987" there is substituted "the Data Protection Act 1998".

Schedules

Tribunals and Inquiries Act 1992 (c. 53)

16. In Part I of Schedule 1 to the Tribunals and Inquiries Act 1992 (tribunals under direct supervision of Council on Tribunals), for paragraph 14 there is substituted—

"Data protection	14.(a) The Data Protection Commissioner appointed under section 6 of the Data Protection Act 1998;
	(b) the Data Protection Tribunal constituted under that section, in respect of its jurisdiction under section 48 of that Act."

Access to Health Records (Northern Ireland) Order 1993 (1993/1250 (N.I. 4))

17. For paragraphs (1) and (2) of Article 4 of the Access to Health Records (Northern Ireland) Order 1993 there is substituted—

"(1) In this Order "health professional" has the same meaning as in the Data Protection Act 1998."

18. In Article 5(4) of that Order (cases where fee may be required) in sub-paragraph (a), for "the maximum prescribed under section 21 of the Data Protection Act 1984" there is substituted "such maximum as may be prescribed for the purposes of this Article by regulations under section 7 of the Data Protection Act 1998".

19. In Article 7 of that Order (cases where right of access may be partially excluded) for the words from the beginning to "record" in the first place where it occurs there is substituted "Access shall not be given under Article 5(2) to any part of a health record".

SCHEDULE 16

Section 74(2)

REPEALS AND REVOCATIONS

PART I

REPEALS

Chapter	Short title	Extent of repeal
1984 c. 35.	The Data Protection Act 1984.	The whole Act.
1986 c. 60.	The Financial Services Act 1986.	Section 190.
1987 c. 37.	The Access to Personal Files Act 1987.	The whole Act.
1988 c. 40.	The Education Reform Act 1988.	Section 223.
1988 c. 50.	The Housing Act 1988.	In Schedule 17, paragraph 80.
1990 c. 23.	The Access to Health Records Act 1990.	In section 1(1), the words from "but does not" to the end.
		In section 3, subsection (1)(a) to (e) and, in subsection (6)(a), the words "in the case of an application made otherwise than by the patient".
		Section 4(1) and (2).
		In section 5(1)(a)(i), the words "of the patient or" and the word "other".
		In section 10, in subsection (2) the words "or orders" and in subsection (3) the words "or an order under section 2(3)

113

		above". In section 11, the definitions of "child" and "parental responsibility".
1990 c. 37.	The Human Fertilisation and Embryology Act 1990.	Section 33(8).
1990 c. 41.	The Courts and Legal Services Act 1990.	In Schedule 10, paragraph 58.
1992 c. 13.	The Further and Higher Education Act 1992.	Section 86.
1992 c. 37.	The Further and Higher Education (Scotland) Act 1992.	Section 59.
1993 c. 8.	The Judicial Pensions and Retirement Act 1993.	In Schedule 6, paragraph 50.
1993 c. 10.	The Charities Act 1993.	Section 12.
1993 c. 21.	The Osteopaths Act 1993.	Section 38.
1994 c. 17.	The Chiropractors Act 1994.	Section 38.
1994 c. 19.	The Local Government (Wales) Act 1994.	In Schedule 13, paragraph 30.
1994 c. 33.	The Criminal Justice and Public Order Act 1994.	Section 161.
1994 c. 39.	The Local Government etc. (Scotland) Act 1994.	In Schedule 13, paragraph 154.

PART II

REVOCATIONS

Number	Title	Extent of revocation
S.I. 1991/1142.	The Data Protection Registration Fee Order 1991.	The whole Order.
S.I. 1991/1707 (N.I. 14).	The Access to Personal Files and Medical Reports (Northern Ireland) Order 1991.	Part II. The Schedule.
S.I. 1992/3218.	The Banking Co-ordination (Second Council Directive) Regulations 1992.	In Schedule 10, paragraphs 15 and 40.
S.I. 1993/1250 (N.I. 4).	The Access to Health Records (Northern Ireland) Order 1993.	In Article 2(2), the definitions of "child" and "parental responsibility". In Article 3(1), the words from "but does not include" to the end. In Article 5, paragraph (1)(a) to (d) and, in paragraph (6)(a), the words "in the case of an application made otherwise than by the patient". Article 6(1) and (2). In Article 7(1)(a)(i), the words "of the patient or" and the word "other".
S.I. 1994/429 (N.I. 2).	The Health and Personal Social Services (Northern Ireland) Order 1994.	In Schedule 1, the entries relating to the Access to Personal Files and Medical Reports (Northern Ireland) Order 1991.
S.I. 1994/1696.	The Insurance Companies (Third Insurance Directives) Regulations 1994.	In Schedule 8, paragraph 8.
S.I. 1995/755 (N.I. 2).	The Children (Northern Ireland) Order 1995.	In Schedule 9, paragraphs 177 and 191.

S.I. 1995/3275.	The Investment Services Regulations 1995.	In Schedule 10, paragraphs 3 and 15.
S.I. 1996/2827.	The Open-Ended Investment Companies (Investment Companies with Variable Capital) Regulations 1996.	In Schedule 8, paragraphs 3 and 26.

NOTES ON STATUTORY INSTRUMENTS

THE DATA PROTECTION ACT 1998 (COMMENCEMENT) ORDER 2000

(S.I. 2000 No. 183 (C.4))

This Order brought the Data Protection Act 1998 into force on March 1, 2000 with the exception of section 56 and those provisions brought into force previously by virtue of section 75(2). Sections 112, 113 and 115 of the Police Act 1997 must be enforced before section 56 (prohibition of requirement as to production of certain records) can be brought into force.

Transitional provision is made under this Order for ongoing requests to credit reference agencies pursuant to section 158 of the Consumer Credit Act 1974.

THE DATA PROTECTION (CORPORATE FINANCE EXEMPTION) ORDER 2000

(S.I. 2000 No. 184)

Data controllers are under an obligation to give each data subject information about the processing of personal data and also to give access to any personal data held about data subjects. Section 27(2) of the Act refers to these obligations as "the subject information provisions". An exemption is contained in paragraph 6 of Schedule 7 to the Act in that data controllers are not required to comply with these obligations where the processing is for the purpose of safeguarding an important economic or financial interest of the United Kingdom.

In considering whether the exemption from the subject information provisions is required for the purpose of safeguarding an important economic or financial interest of the United Kingdom, the Order provides that the inevitable prejudicial effect on the orderly functioning of financial markets for the efficient allocation of capital within the economy resulting from the occasional or regular application of the subject information provisions must be taken into account. The personal data in question are data that, if disclosed, would affect decisions whether to deal in, subscribe for or issue instruments for decisions that are likely to affect any business activity.

THE DATA PROTECTION (CONDITIONS UNDER PARAGRAPH 3 OF PART II OF SCHEDULE 1) ORDER 2000

(S.I. 2000 No. 185)

Paragraph 2 of Part II of Schedule 1 to the Data Protection Act 1998 provides that personal data will not be treated as processed fairly unless certain requirements are met relating to the provision to the data subject of the information about the processing ("the information requirement"). Different provisions apply depending on whether data have been obtained from the data subject or from some other third party.

Paragraph 3 of Part II of Schedule 1 sets out conditions which allow the data controller exemption from the information requirements in cases where the data have been obtained from a source other than the data subject.

Article 4 of the Order sets out further conditions for cases where the disproportionate effort found in paragraph 3(2)(a) of Part II of Schedule 1 is being relied upon, or where the disclosure or recording of the data is necessary for compliance of the legal obligation, other than one imposed by contact or by or under an enactment or by a court order. This Order provides that any data controller must still provide the relevant information to any individual who requests it despite the fact that the data controller is claiming the benefit of the disapplication of the information requirements. If a data controller does not have sufficient information about the individual in order to determine whether he is processing personal data about that individual, the data controller is still obliged to send the individual a written notice explaining the position.

Article 5 of the Order provides that a data controller must give a record of the reasons why he believes disapplication of the information requirements is necessary.

THE DATA PROTECTION (FUNCTIONS OF DESIGNATED AUTHORITY) ORDER 2000

(S.I. 2000 No. 186)

Section 54(1) of the Data Protection Act 1998 provides that the Information Commissioner will continue to be the designated authority in the United Kingdom for the purposes of Article 13 of the Convention for the Protection of Individuals with regard to Automatic Processing of Personal Data. Section 54(2) provides that the Secretary of State may by Order make provision as to the functions to be discharged by the Information Commissioner in that capacity.

The Order sets out those functions. In terms of Article 3, the Information Commissioner must furnish particular information to the designated authorities in other convention countries and he may request those other authorities to furnish him with information. The Information Commissioner must assist persons resident outside the United Kingdom in exercising certain of their rights under Part II of the Act. If the Information Commissioner receives a request for assistance in exercising rights of access to personal data in a convention country by a person resident in the United Kingdom, the Information Commissioner will send the request to the designated authority in that country.

THE DATA PROTECTION (FEES UNDER SECTION 19(7)) REGULATIONS 2000

(S.I. 2000 No. 187)

The Regulations set out that a fee of £2 must be paid to the Information Commissioner for a certified copy of a data controller's entry on the register.

THE DATA PROTECTION (NOTIFICATION AND NOTIFICATION FEES) REGULATIONS 2000

(S.I. 2000 No. 188)

The Regulations deal with the giving of notifications to the Information Commissioner by data controllers under Part III of the Data Protection Act 1998.

Data controllers carrying out certain processing are exempt from the need to notify in terms of regulation 3. The exempt processing operations are set out in the Schedule to the Regulations, and cover processing operations involving staff administration, advertising, marketing, public relations, accounts and record keeping and certain processing operations carried out by non-profit making organisations. If the processing falls within the description of accessible processing certified by the Secretary of State under section 22 of the Act, then the notification exemption is lost.

The Information Commissioner can determine the form of notification under regulation 4. Cases where there is more than one data controller in respect of personal data are covered by regulations 5 and 6. Regulation 5 provides for the notification by business partners to be in the name of partnership and regulation 6 for notification of the governing body and head teacher of the school to be in the name of the school.

A fee of £35 is prescribed under regulation 7 to accompany a notification under section 18 of the Act.

Regulation 8 deals with time or receipt of notification.

If the Information Commissioner considers a notification that he has received relates to accessible processing in the meaning of section 22 of the Act, the Information Commissioner must give written notice to a data controller within 10 days of receipt of the notification. The date of receipt and the processing considered to be accessible must also be stated.

The Information Commissioner must give notice to a data controller confirming his register entry under regulation 10. The notice must be given as soon as practicable and in any event within 28 days of making a register entry under section 19 of the Act or of amending it under section 20. The confirmation must also share the date on which the entry is deemed in terms of regulation 8 to have been made or, if an alteration to an entry, the date of the alteration.

The Information Commissioner is authorised to include certain matters in a register entry in addition to the registrable particulars set out in section 16 of the Act. Those matters are a registration number, the deemed date of entry provided by regulation 8, the date on which the entry may lapse under regulations 14 or 15, and additional information for the purpose of assisting communication about data protection matters between persons consulting the register and the data controller.

Every data controller who has a register entry is under a duty to notify the Information Commissioner if the entry becomes an inaccurate or incomplete statement of his current registrable particulars or on which the latest description of security matters given under section 18(2)(b) of the Act becomes inaccurate or incomplete. The notification must set out the changes that need to be made to ensure accuracy and completeness and must be given as soon as practicable and in any event within 28 days from the time when the inaccuracy or incompleteness arises. The duty under regulation 12 varies according to the extent to which the entry relates to data that are subject to processing already under way immediately before October 24, 1998. In respect of such data, the notification must specify certain aspects of processing which are not from time to time included in the existing register entry. In other cases it must specify an entry that becomes inaccurate or incomplete in certain respects and set out the changes needed to ensure accuracy and completeness.

The fee to be paid annually to secure retention of a registered entry is £35 set out in regulation 14.

THE DATA PROTECTION TRIBUNAL (ENFORCEMENT APPEALS) RULES 2000

(S.I. 2000 No. 189)

These rules regulate the exercise of the rights of appeal against decisions of the Information Commissioner conferred by section 48 of the Act and the practice and procedure of the Data Protection Tribunal in such cases. An appeal must be made by notice of appeal served on the Tribunal, stating the grounds of appeal and any other specified particulars with provision for including a request with reasons for an early hearing. An appeal against an information notice may also include representations against a hearing by the chairman or deputy sitting alone.

Rule 4 provides that the notice must be served within 28 days of the date on which the Information Commissioner's decision was served on the appellant, although appeals may be accepted out of time in special circumstances. The notice of the appeal must be acknowledged and a copy served on the Information Commissioner except in the case of certain appeals to be heard *ex parte*. The Information Commissioner may make a reply in terms of rule 6.

The Information Commissioner can apply for an appeal to be struck out in limited circumstances set out in rule 7. Parties can amend their pleadings and rule 9 makes provision in respect of the withdrawal of an appeal. Rule 10 allows for the consolidation of appeal.

Rule 11 provides for the giving of directions by the Tribunal, of its own motion or on the application of a party and this power may be exercised in the absence of the parties. Any party may apply to set aside or vary direction. Persons can be ordered to permit entry for the testing of equipment or material connected with the processing of personal data.

Generally the Tribunal must proceed by way of a hearing although rule 13 provides that it may determine an appeal without a hearing in certain circumstances. Provision is made as to the appointment of time and place of a hearing (rule 14), summoning of witnesses to attend a hearing (rule 15), representation at a hearing (rule 16) and default of appearance at a hearing (rule 17). The constitution of the Tribunal for hearing certain appeals against an information notice is set out in rule 18.

Although hearings by the Tribunal must be in public, special provision is made for hearings to be heard in private in limited circumstances. These rules are the provision as to the conduct of proceedings at a hearing (rule 20), powers of the chairman to act for the tribunal (rule 21), evidence (rule 23), determination of appeals (rule 24), and costs (rule 25). The onus is placed on the Information Commissioner to satisfy the Tribunal that his decision should be upheld under the acceptance of those proceedings relating to the inclusion of a statement of urgency in the Information Commissioner's notice.

THE DATA PROTECTION (INTERNATIONAL CO-OPERATION) ORDER 2000

(S.I. 2000 No. 190)

Section 54(3) of the Act provides that the Secretary of State may by Order make provision as to the co-operation between the Information Commissioner, the European Commission and other supervisory authorities in EEA States. In terms of this Order, the Information Commissioner is obliged to give to the European Commission and supervisory authorities his reasons for being satisfied that a transfer or proposed transfer of personal data has involved or would involve a transfer to a country or territory outside the EEA which has inadequate protection for the rights and freedoms of data subjects in relation to the processing of personal data, and would be a breach of the eighth protection principle in Part I of Schedule 1.

The enforcement powers of the Information Commissioner under Part V of the Act are extended so that they can be exercised in relation to certain data controllers who are processing data in the United Kingdom although the Act does not apply by virtue of section 5 of the Act. The Information Commissioner can exercise these powers following a request from the supervisory authority of the EEA State. The Information Commissioner can make similar requests for assistance where a data controller falling within the scope of the Information Commissioner's functions is processing data in another EEA State.

The Information Commissioner is also entitled to supply other information to the European Commission or supervisory authorities if that information is necessary for the discharge of their data protection functions.

THE DATA PROTECTION (SUBJECT ACCESS) (FEES AND MISCELLANEOUS PROVISIONS) REGULATIONS 2000

(S.I. 2000 No. 191)

These Regulations make provision in respect of the exercise of the right of access to personal data in terms of section 7 of the Act.

A request for access to information under any provision of section 7(1)(a) to (c) is treated as extending to all information. However, a request is not to be taken to extend to information about the logic of automated decision taking under section 7(1)(d) unless an express intention appears and if there is an express intention, the request is to be treated as limited to that information unless an express contrary intention appears.

The maximum fee that the data controller can charge for access to data under section 7(2) is £10 except in the special cases set out in regulations 4, 5 and 6.

Special provision as to fees and time limits in relation to three particular types of subject access requests are set out in the regulations as follows:

(1) Where the data controller is a credit reference agency and a subject access request is limited to personal data relevant to the applicant's financial standing, the maximum fee for access is £2. The time period within which the data controller must comply with the request is seven working days.

(2) Where the subject access request relates to accessible records that are education records, no access fee may be charged unless a permanent copy of the information is to be provided. In this case the maximum fee which may be charged for access is set out in the schedule to the Regulations and varies according to the type and volume of copies. The time period for compliance with these requests is fifteen school days in England and Wales or forty days in any other circumstances.

(3) The Regulations made transitional provision in respect of certain requests made before October 24, 2001. These requests were subject access requests relating to accessible records that were health records and that were not exclusively automated or intended for automation. Where a permanent copy of the information was to be provided, the maximum fee that could be charged by the data controller was £50. Where the request was restricted solely to data that formed part of a health record and that record had been partially created within the forty days preceding the request and no copy of the information was to be provided, no fee was allowed to be charged.

THE DATA PROTECTION TRIBUNAL (NATIONAL SECURITY APPEALS) RULES 2000

(S.I. 2000 No. 206)

Section 28 of the Act relates to the certification by a Minister that exemption from provisions of the Act is or was required for the purpose of safeguarding national security. These rules regulate the exercise of the rights of appeal conferred by this section and the practice and procedure of the Data Protection Tribunal in such cases.

There is a general duty on the Tribunal in such cases to secure that such information is not disclosed contrary to the interest of national security. The ex parte jurisdiction of the Tribunal to matters concerning the summary disposal of appeals under rule 11 is also limited.

An appeal must be made by notice of appeal served on the Tribunal stating the grounds of appeal and other specified particulars. Time limits for appealing are set out in rule 5. The appeal must be acknowledged. The Minister who signed the certificate can reply to a notice in terms of rule 7 and rule 8 provides for reply by the data controller in section 28(6) cases claiming the application of the certificate. Parties can amend their pleadings in terms of rule 9. The Minister or the data controller can apply to the Tribunal for an appeal to be struck out in certain circumstances. The Tribunal, if it considers it proper to do so, can dismiss an appeal on the basis of consideration of the notice of appeal, the minister's notice and any reply by the data controller. The expellant, however, is entitled to make representations written and oral against a proposal to deal with the appeal under this procedure before the Tribunal can dismiss such an appeal.

The Minister can object on grounds of national security to the disclosure of his notice and reply, or any data controller's reply, to a party or the Information Commissioner. The Minister in question must give reasons and if possible supply a version of the notice that can be disclosed and the procedure set out in rule 17 applies to the objections.

Provision is also made in respect of the withdrawal of an appeal and the consolidation of appeal.

The Minister is able to reply on national security grounds for the Tribunal to consider proposals to exercise certain of its powers.

Generally the Tribunal must proceed by way of a hearing within certain additional circumstances that determine an appeal without a hearing.

Hearings by the Tribunal must be in private although provision is made for a public hearing and the admission of other persons in limited circumstances.

THE CONSUMER CREDIT (CREDIT REFERENCE AGENCY) REGULATIONS 2000

(S.I. 2000 No. 290)

These Regulations revoke most of the provisions of the Consumer Credit (Credit Reference Agency) Regulations 1977 and supplement section 9(3) of the Data Protection Act 1998 as well as sections 157 to 160 of the Consumer Credit Act 1974.

With regard to section 9(3) of the Data Protection Act 1998, the Regulations prescribe the detailed form which the statements supplied by credit reference agencies should take when advising individuals of their rights under section 159 of the 1974 Act. The prescribed form incorporates a statement of certain rights under the Data Protection Act 1998.

There are two kinds of application that must be made in a manner prescribed by the Regulations, and these are:

(1) applications by an individual and other consumers to the Information Commissioner or the Director General of Fair Trading ("the relevant authority") for an order where a credit reference agency has not given notice that it intends to include a notice of correction drawn up by the consumer on its files; and

(2) applications by credit reference agencies to the relevant authority where they think it would be improper to include such a notice of correction on their files.

THE DATA PROTECTION (SUBJECT ACCESS MODIFICATION) (HEALTH) ORDER 2000

(S.I. 2000 No. 413)

This Order provides for the partial exemption from the provisions of the Act that confer rights on data subjects to gain access to data held about them where the data relates to the physical or mental health or condition of the data subject.

Personal data are exempt from section 7 only when its application would be likely to cause serious harm to the health or medical condition of the data subject or any other person. The provisions in the Order also cover data controllers who are not health professionals. Before making a determination as to whether this exemption applies, a data controller who is not a health professional is under an obligation to consult the health professional who is responsible for the care of the data subject. If there is more than one health professional then the most suitable health professional should be consulted. If there are no health professionals available, or if the data controller is the Secretary of State exercising his functions in relation to social security, child support or war pensions, a health professional must be consulted who has the necessary experience to advise on the matter in question. If the data subject has already seen or knows about the information which is the subject of the request or if a consultation has been carried out prior to the request being made, then the obligation to consult does not apply.

If a third party makes a request for access to data on behalf of a data subject against the data subject's wishes, then a further exemption from section 7 is conferred.

A data controller cannot refuse access to health records on the grounds that the identity of a third party would be disclosed if that third party is a health professional who has dealt with the data subject in a professional capacity or contributed to a health record. However, the data controller can refuse access if serious harm to that health professional's physical or mental health or condition is likely to be caused by giving such access.

THE DATA PROTECTION (SUBJECT ACCESS MODIFICATION) (EDUCATION) ORDER 2000

(S.I. 2000 No. 414)

This Order applies to access to personal data relating to "educational records" (defined in Schedule 11, paragraph 1) and provides for the partial exemption from the provisions of the Act that confers rights on data subjects to access data held about them where that data are "education records". There must be the likelihood that the exercise of rights of access to these records would cause serious harm to the physical or mental health or condition of the data subject or another person. In some circumstances (except in Scotland), the exemption does not apply where the data subject is or has been the subject of or may be at the risk of child abuse as the disclosure would not be in the best interests of the data subject. The Order does not apply to any data covered by the Data Protection (Subject Access Modification) (Health) Order 2000 or by an order made under section 38(1) of the Act.

Section 7 of the Act is modified so that a data controller cannot refuse access on the grounds that the identity of a third party would be disclosed if that third party is a relevant person defined in article 7(2), unless serious harm to that relevant person's physical or mental health or condition is likely to be caused. A "relevant person" is defined as:

(a) an employee of the local education authority which maintains the school;

(b) a teacher or employee of a special school or a school not maintained by the local education authority;

(c) a teacher at the school;

(d) an employee of an education and library board other than a teacher;

(e) an employee of an education authority in pursuance of its functions relating to education; or

(f) the person making the request.

In the case of data controllers that are education authorities in Scotland and receive certain data from the Principal Reporter, the Order requires such data controllers to obtain the opinion of the Principal Reporter before responding to a section 7 request as to whether the disclosure of the information might cause serious harm to anyone.

THE DATA PROTECTION (SUBJECT ACCESS MODIFICATION) (SOCIAL WORK) ORDER 2000

(S.I. 2000 No. 415)

This Order provides for the partial exemption from the provisions of the Act that confer rights on data subjects to gain access to personal data where the exercise of access rights would be likely to prejudice the carrying out of social work functions by causing serious harm to the physical or mental condition of the data subject or another person. The Order does not apply to any data covered by the Data Protection (Subject Access Modification) (Health) Order 2000, the Data Protection (Subject Access Modification) (Education) Order 2000 or by an order made under section 38(1) of the Act.

Section 7 of the Act is modified in that a data controller cannot refuse access on the grounds that the identity of a third party would be disclosed if that third party is a "relevant person", unless serious harm to that relevant person's physical or mental condition is likely to be caused by giving access. "Relevant person" is defined in the Order as:

(a) a guardian *ad litem*;

(b) the Principal Reporter; or

(c) an employee of any person or body referred to in paragraph 1 of the Schedule to this Order.

Where a third party makes a request for access to data on behalf of a data subject against the data subject's wishes, this is also exempt from section 7.

Paragraph 1 of the Schedule annexed to the Order ensures that the Order principally applies to data which are processed by local authorities in their social services and education welfare functions, health authorities, probation committees and the National Society for the Prevention of Cruelty to Children. Other voluntary organisations or other bodies can be added to the list where the data are processed for purposes similar to the social services functions of local authorities.

THE DATA PROTECTION (CROWN APPOINTMENTS) ORDER 2000

(S.I. 2000 No. 416)

Data controllers are under an obligation to give data subjects information about the processing of their personal data and access to the personal data. The "subject information provisions" are referred to in section 27(2) of the Act.

This Order exempts from the subject information provisions processing of personal data for the purposes of assessing any person's suitability for certain offices to which appointments are made by Her Majesty.

THE DATA PROTECTION (PROCESSING OF SENSITIVE PERSONAL DATA) ORDER 2000

(S.I. 2000 No. 417)

The first data protection principle states that the processing of sensitive personal data is prohibited unless one of the conditions in Schedule 3 to the Act is met.

Paragraph 10 of that Schedule states that the Secretary of State can specify circumstances where the processing of sensitive personal data can be carried out. The Schedule to this Order specifies such circumstances.

These circumstances are:

(1) That the processing is in the substantial public interest or is necessary for the purposes of the prevention or detection of any unlawful acts and where obtaining the explicit consent of the data subject would prejudice those purposes.

(2) The processing is in the substantial public interest or is necessary for the discharge of any function designed to protect members of the public against dishonesty, malpractice, mismanagement in the administration of services provided by anybody, etc. and must be carried out without the explicit consent of the data subject so as not to prejudice the discharge of that function.

(3) The disclosure of personal data is for journalistic, artistic or literary purposes relating to a wide range of conduct, *e.g.* unlawful acts, dishonesty and incompetence, etc.

(4) The processing is necessary to carry out confidential counselling advice and support and requires to be carried out without the explicit consent of the data subject because the consent cannot be given by the data subject, the data controller cannot reasonably be expected to obtain the consent or the obtaining of consent would prejudice the provision of the counselling.

(5) Where processing is being carried out for insurance or pensions purposes and details of particular relatives of the principal insured or member are required, the data controller must not process the relative's personal data to make decisions or take actions in respect of the relatives. He is also unable to process the relative's personal data if the data controller is aware that the relative is withholding his consent to the processing.

(6) Processing of sensitive personal data for insurance or pensions schemes carried out before the Order came into force cannot be continued if the data controller is aware of the data subject withholding his consent to the processing. The data controller may continue the processing in the case of group insurance or pension schemes without the explicit consent of the data subject to avoid prejudice to that insurance policy or pension scheme.

(7) Processing of information about political opinions by registered political parties can be carried out provided that the processing does not cause substantial damage or distress any persons.

Processing by the police in exercise of their common law powers is also covered by the Order.

THE DATA PROTECTION (MISCELLANEOUS SUBJECT ACCESS EXEMPTIONS) ORDER 2000

(S.I. 2000 No. 419)

This Statutory Instrument has been significantly amended with respect to adoption regulations by the Data Protection (Miscellaneous Subject Access Exemptions) (Amendment) Order 2000 (S.I. 2000 No. 1865).

THE DATA PROTECTION (DESIGNATED CODES OF PRACTICE) (NO. 2) ORDER 2000

(S.I. 2000 No. 1864)

This Statutory Instrument has been made to correct a defect in S.I. 2000 No. 418 and therefore revokes and replaces it. The original Order referred to each code by reference to the date of issue, but in relation to one code the date of issue referred to has been superseded by a subsequent issue by the date on which the Order was made. This Order therefore does not refer to dates of issue.

For the purposes of section 32(3) of the Act, article 2 of this Order designates the codes of practice that are listed in the Schedule to the Order. Compliance with any of the designated codes may be taken into account when considering, for the purposes of section 32(1)(b) of the Act, the reasonableness of the belief of a data controller that the publication of any journalistic, literary or artistic material would be in the public interest.

THE DATA PROTECTION (MISCELLANEOUS SUBJECT ACCESS EXEMPTIONS) (AMENDMENT) ORDER 2000

(S.I. 2000 No. 1865)

This Order has been made to correct a defect in S.I. 2000 No. 419 which exempts from section 7 of the Act personal data, the disclosure of which is prohibited or restricted by certain enactments and subordinate instruments in the interests of safeguarding the interests of the data subject himself or the rights and freedoms of some other individual.

The previous Order exempted personal data that included information contained in adoption records and reports. Disclosure of information which is prohibited or restricted by regulations 6 and 14 of the Adoption Agencies Regulations 1983 or by regulation 23 of the Adoption Agencies (Scotland) Regulations 1996 is limited by the previous Order with regard to records and other information in the possession of local authorities. However, for the purposes of both sets of Regulations, an approved adoption society is an adoption agency. This Order amends the previous Order by removing the limitation to allow the exemption to apply whether or not the adoption agency possessing the records or information is a local authority.

INDEX

References are to sections and Schedules

Index

DATA SUBJECTS—*cont.*
 children in Scotland, exercise of rights
  by, 66
 compensation, 13
 consent of, Sched.2
 credit reference agencies, where data
  controllers are, 7
 destruction, 14
 direct marketing, right to prevent, 11
 erasure, 14
 exempt manual data, 12A
 exemptions, Sched.8
 interpretation, 1
 jurisdiction, 15
 legitimate interests, Sched.2
 personal data, rights of access to, 7
 records, 56
 rectification, 14
 rights of, 7–15, 56, Sched.14
 Scotland, children in, 66
DEFINITIONS
 accessible records, 68
 data, 1
 data processors, 1
 health professionals, 69
 index of defined expressions, 71
 processing, 1
 relevant filing system, 1
 special purpose, 3
 supplementary, 70
DESTRUCTION OF DATA, 14
DIRECT MARKETING, 11
DIRECTOR GENERAL OF FAIR TRADING,
 31
DIRECTORS
 liability of, 61
DOMESTIC PURPOSES EXEMPTION, 36
DURATION OF RETENTION OF DATA,
 Sched.1

EC LAW
 confidentiality, 59
 data protection principles, Sched.1
 Information Commissioner, 51
EDUCATION, 30, Sched.11, App.
ELECTRONIC TRANSMISSION OF NOTICES,
 64
ENACTMENT
 information available under, 39
ENFORCEMENT, 40–50, Sched.1
 appeals, 40–41, 48–49, App.
 assessments, request for, 42
 cancellation of notices, 41
 data protection principles, 40
 entry, powers of, 50, Sched.9
 information notices, 43, 44, 47–48
 inspection, powers of, 50, Sched.9
 investigations, 40
 notices, 40–41, 43, 44
  appeals, 48–49
  failure to comply with, 47
 special information notices, 44,
  47–48

ENFORCEMENT—*cont.*
 special purposes,
  determination by Information
   Commissioner as to, 45
  restrictions on enforcement, 46
 transitional provisions, Sched.14
 warrants, issue and execution of,
  Sched.9
ENTRY
 powers of, 50, Sched.9
ERASURE OF DATA, 14
EUROPEAN ECONOMIC AREA, 1, 4, 51,
 Sched.1, Sched.4
EXAMINATION MARKS AND SCRIPTS,
 Sched.7
EXEMPTIONS, 27–39, Sched.7
 accounts, Sched.8
 armed forces, Sched.7
 automated data, Sched.8
 art, 32
 back-up data, Sched.8
 confidentiality, Sched.7
 corporate finance, Sched.7, App.
 crime, 29
 Crown or ministerial appointments,
  Sched.7
 data protection principles, 27
 data subject, processing other than by
  reference to, Sched.8
 Director General of Fair Trading, 31
 domestic purposes, 36
 education, 30, App.
 enactment, information available
  under, 34
 examination marks and scripts,
  Sched.7
 health, 30, App.
 history, 33
 journalism, 32
 judicial appointments and honours,
  Sched.7
 legal proceedings or law, disclosure
  required by, 35
 legal professional privilege, Sched.7
 literature, 32
 mailing lists, Sched.8
 management forecasts, Sched.7
 manual data, 12A, Sched.8, Sched.13
 national security, 28, App.
 negotiations, Sched.7
 order, power to make further
  exemptions by, 38
 payroll, Sched.8
 public, information available to, 34
 regulatory activity, 31
 references, Sched.7
 research, 33, Sched.8
 seizure, Sched.9
 self-incrimination, Sched.7
 social work, 30, App.
 statistics, 33
 taxation, 28
 transitional relief, 39

140